THE ROAD TO TANGANYIKA

D1196415

Copyright 2006 James McCarthy (ed.)

Published by
Kachere Series
P.O. Box 1037, Zomba
ISBN 99908-76-45-2 Kachere Text no. 23

The Kachere Series is represented outside Africa by:
African Books Collective, Oxford (orders@africanbookscollective.com)
Michigan State University Press, East Lansing (msupress@msu.edu)

Layout and Cover: Mercy Chilunga
Graphic Design: Patrick Lichakala

Printed in Malawi by Assemblies of God Press, P.O. Box 5749, Limbe.

THE ROAD TO TANGANYIKA

The Diaries of Donald Munro
and William McEwan of the Stevenson Road

With an Introduction and Explanatory Notes

Edited by James McCarthy

Kachere Text no. 23
Kachere Series
Zomba
2006

Series Editor's Preface

The Kachere tree is a local Malawian variety of the fig tree, and since it grows so big, that it provides much shade, it is a preferred tree for meetings. When Chief Kapeni in Blantyre welcomed the missionaries, they found many Kachere trees at his residence, and when Dr David Livingstone met the chiefs of Nkhota Kota, they met under a Kachere tree. When missionaries, black or white, opened their schools, they often chose to do so under a Kachere tree. That may not be the rule anymore, so we invite you to sit under our virtual Kachere tree and read dour real books and discuss with anyone who wants to share.

The Kachere Series is an initiative of the Department of Theology and Religious Studies at the University of Malawi. It was begun in 1995 with the aim of promoting the emergence of a body of literature to engage critically with religion in Malawi, its social and political impact and the theological questions it raises. By now the Kachere Series has over eighty publications, and while it still has its original aim, it has widened its remit to include fields other than religion like poetry, ecology, history or literary criticism. Most books deal *with* Malawi, but some just come *from* Malawi, but we believe that all may be useful both within Malawi and without.

In the beginning the Kachere Series had three sub-series: *Kachere Books* had a more general appeal, *Kachere Texts* were the mixed bag for smaller and unusual contributions, and the *Kachere Monographs* were the prestigious third branch, for which only full-length academic treatises based on solid primary research were accepted. Later the *Kachere Studies* were added, which provide room for works not necessarily dealing with Malawi, *Kachere Theses* which are similar to monographs, and the *Mvunguti Series* which mainly caters for books in Malawian languages other than English. Lately *Kachere Tools* (for teaching and learning) were added and the *Sources for the Study of Religion in Malawi* were revived to provide an outlet for research results below the monograph level.

As editors we are happy to present this Kachere Book to document the achievements and struggles to establish a modern road network in Malawi. We are also keen to present the books as documenting the interface between development and missionary work in the early period of European contact, as the work on the Stevenson Road was initiated by Scottish philanthropical interests, in close vicinity to both the Livingstonia Mission and the African Lakes Company.

Kachere Series Editors
January 2006

Foreword

I first came across the names of Donald Munro and William McEwan thirty years ago, when I was researching in the National Library of Scotland in Edinburgh, into the early history of the Livingstonia Mission. Day after day I was reading slowly through large letter-books, filled with hundreds of letters and reports sent back to Scotland from what is now Malawi to the headquarters of the Free Church of Scotland. Although it is now more than a quarter of a century ago, I still remember clearly the emotional shock of turning a page in one of these letter-books for 1885, and finding a telegram announcing the sudden death from fever of William O. McEwan. For a few moments the unexpected news hit me as if I had known him personally, for when you research deeply into the correspondence of such nineteenth century pioneers, they begin to come alive for you, and you feel that they are people that you yourself have met.

One reason for this is that the Scots were particularly good at keeping diaries and journals, and in writing back home—both to family and in a more official capacity—so that a considerable amount of information about them is still available. In Edinburgh University alone, we have diaries, journals and photographs from Robert Laws, A.G. MacAlpine, and Joseph Booth (all closely connected to Malawi) and only a few days before I began writing this, another Malawi missionary diary belonging to Alexander Dewar (who worked at both Livingstonia and Mwenzo) went up for auction at Sotheby's in London. Fortunately, New College Library, Edinburgh, was successful in bidding for it, so that yet another important source of Scottish missionary writing about Malawi will be made available for researchers. Dewar's diary is illustrative of the detail with which these Scottish missionaries wrote about what was going on around them. It is in seven volumes, spread over fourteen years, and runs to over nine hundred pages in all.

Such diaries and journals can give us much interesting and useful information that is often not available in other forms, for they are immediate, instinctive reactions to people and events, and are normally personal and private – not intended for public reading. They are, therefore, often much more honest about colleagues and situations than letters or reports would be. They also sometimes provide interesting sidelights into the ideas and interests of those writing them. William McEwan, (and to a lesser extent, Donald Munro) for example, tells us what he reads each day. This ranges across several fields –

religion, science, and politics. Taken together with similar information from other journals and diaries it helps historians to build up a better picture of the literary sources which helped to form the opinions of Scottish missionaries in Africa in the late nineteenth century.

One particular reason why the diaries of Donald Munro and William McEwan are of interest is that they neatly complement that of James Stewart CE, which I published in 1989 under the title of *From Nyassa to Tanganyika*. James Stewart, the civil engineer, was the cousin of the more famous Dr. James Stewart of Lovedale, who, among other things, had suggested the setting up of the Livingstonia mission in memory of David Livingstone, and who worked in Malawi – mostly at Cape Maclear – in 1876 and 1877. The younger James Stewart came to visit his cousin during a period of leave from his work in India, and stayed in Malawi to help lay out the basic plans for Blantyre, to explore a possible route for a road between lakes Nyasa and Tanganyika, and later, to begin actual construction work on the road. When James Stewart CE died of fever in August 1883, while working on the construction of the Stevenson Road with Donald Munro, he was replaced by a young Glasgow engineer by the name of William O McEwan, who subsequently depended greatly on the more experienced Munro.

As James McCarthy points out in his Introduction, two of the three parts of McEwan's diary have already been published. For those with an interest in Malawi however, the third unpublished part is of most importance, for it deals with the last portion of William McEwan's life – his arrival in what is now Malawi, his interaction with many of the personalities central to James Stewart's earlier journal, his reaching the site of the Stevenson Road, his attempts to continue the work begun by Stewart and his colleague Munro, his meeting with Swahili slave traders such as Mlozi, and (of particular interest to me in my present research) his experiments with photography.

Diaries such as those of Munro and McEwan, which James McCarthy brings to us in this book, are full of small details which are often not important in themselves. When we say that McEwan tells us what he had for breakfast, we are not using a metaphor: he actually does! Yet such works are important in another sense. They are like finding a box with missing pieces of a large jigsaw puzzle which you have been trying to finish for some time. As you take the new pieces and begin to fit them into the picture you already have, that overall picture becomes clearer and more understandable. In spite of the fact that

William McEwan spent a very short time in Malawi, and that he died at a tragically early age, his diary adds to our knowledge of the early missionary period there in the 1880s. James McCarthy is to be congratulated for bringing these diaries to our attention, and for making the Malawi section more widely available for the first time.

Jack Thompson
University of Edinburgh
November 2004

Contents

List of Illustrations

Acknowledgements

I am particularly grateful to Dr. David Munro of the Royal Scottish Geographical Society for drawing my attention to the existence of the McEwan diary in the first instance and for making arrangements for this to be transferred to the National Library of Scotland for my convenience during transcription. I am also indebted to the Maps Library of that institution for holding the diary and to their staff, not only for making it available to me at any time, but also providing facilities for working on their premises.

I had completed this work based exclusively on the McEwan diary, when a newspaper article prompted Munro's granddaughter, Mrs. Amy Mouat, to contact me to let me know of the existence of the Munro diary. Through her kindness and that of her daughter, Jan McCorkindale, arrangements were made to allow me to abstract from this, making the story a much more complete one. They also gave valuable background information on Donald Munro and their helpfulness has been much appreciated.

Donald Munro and his Granddaughter in 1931

Dr. Jack Thompson of New College, Edinburgh commented helpfully on my first draft, and has kindly written a Foreword. At the same institution, I had useful discussions with Rev. Andrew Ross. Colin Willshaw in Malawi kindly allowed me to use his notes on the Stevenson Road and kept me up to date on the condition of that road and the memorial to James Stevenson, while maintaining a continuing interest in this project. Scott Giebel, a one-time Peace Corps volunteer at Chitipa allowed me access to his unpublished notes on the road and its historical background. Mike Shand of Glasgow University pointed me to sources on survey instruments and techniques of the time. My particular thanks to Andrew Gorzalka for converting original illustrations into digitized format.

I am most grateful to the University of Glasgow, the National Library of Scotland, and the Hope Trust for supporting this publication through their generous and prompt sponsorship, and also to the Royal Scottish Geographical Society for financial help.

Finally my thanks to Dr. Klaus Fiedler of the Department of Theology and Religious Studies at the University of Malawi for arranging for this work to be published in the Kachere Series.

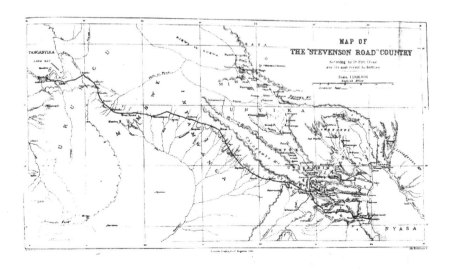

Introduction

While lying in a half feverish condition, trying to doze away the hot noon hours, I was much surprised to hear a strange hubbub. Yelling and shouting and firing of guns suddenly became the order of the day. Thinking that the village had suddenly been attacked by some enemy, I rushed hastily out of my hut, gun in hand: and there to my infinite amazement stood a white man! If he had been a ghost from the tomb I could not have been more astonished, and I seemed like one paralysed. Smilingly, the great unknown came forward. And according to the African salutation a la mode he touched his hat, and said, "Mr. Thomson, I presume?" Recovering myself somewhat, I replied "Yes, that is my name; but good gracious! Who are you?" My name is Stewart" Ah! thought I, a Scotchman, of course!

Thus the 21-year old Scottish explorer Joseph Thomson, having pioneered a route between Lake Nyasa and Lake Tanganyika in 1879 on behalf of the Royal Geographical Society describes his completely unexpected meeting with the civil engineer James Stewart who was to start the construction between these lakes of one of the most famous roads in Africa – the Stevenson Road.

The man who gave his name to the Stevenson Road and dedicated a significant part of his fortune to it was James Stevenson, a successful Glasgow businessman and a partner in the chemical manufacturing firm of Stevenson, Carlile and Co. He obviously came from a relatively wealthy family, since his father was known to be a substantial benefactor to both the Free Church of Scotland and Glasgow University. (He himself owned a sulphur mine on the island of Vulcano off Sicily which was the basis for his chemical works.) Born in 1822, Stevenson was educated at Glasgow University and acquired a number of academic distinctions as a Fellow of both the Royal Geographical Society and the Royal Society of Edinburgh, was awarded an LL.D., and in 1878 was elected Lord Dean of Glasgow at a time when that city, the so-called 'workshop of the world' was considered second only to London in terms of industrial development and commercial enterprise. The family nick-name for this life-long bachelor was Croesus—an indication of his wealth.

As a strong supporter of the Free Church, Stevenson was, like so many of his colleagues, imbued with David Livingstone's ideas of civilising Africa through commerce and the spread of Christianity. He himself had studied the African question in some depth, especially in relation to East and Central Africa and

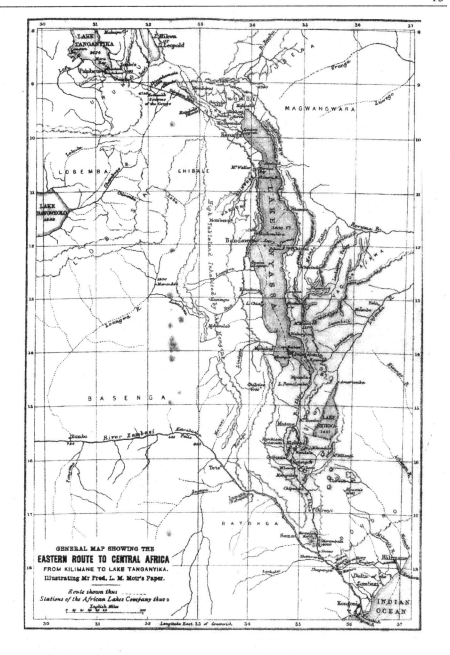

GENERAL MAP SHOWING THE
EASTERN ROUTE TO CENTRAL AFRICA
FROM KILIMANE TO LAKE TANGANYIKA.
Illustrating Mr Fred. L. M. Moir's Paper.

Route shown thus
Stations of the African Lakes Company thus ○
English Miles

wrote a number of papers—the first of these rather grandly entitled *The Civilisation of South Eastern Africa*—which implies a knowledge of these territories although he was not to visit the continent till several years later. (He was in fact a classic example of the so-called 'armchair geographers' who were often derided by field explorers.) These papers focus on a number of inter-related threads in the development of the interior, primarily the need for economic communications, wherever possible utilising the waterways of Central Africa and the curtailment of Arab (a shorthand used at the time for any Muslim traders who were often of mixed blood) and Portuguese influence in this area, linked to the cessation of the slave trade.

Although the slave trade was legally abolished within the British Empire by Thomson's time and had been accepted by the Sultan of Zanzibar in the territory under his jurisdiction, it was still actively pursued in the interior, its effects exacerbated by almost continuous tribal warfare. Fred Moir, one of the managers of the African Lakes Company (ALC) of which Stevenson was chairman, describes country near L. Tanganyika devastated by slavery, which had been well peopled and prosperous only a few years ago:

> '... we found utter desolation; grass ranker in places than on the plains told where cultivation had been, hippopotami and buffaloes had laid waste the banana groves, the doors of the stockade were nearly impassable from thorns and creepers, while within and without, the whitening skulls told of the too common tragedy of Africa, of a fair and smiling country turned at one fell swoop to a grave and a ruin by the grasping avarice of some fiend in human shape.'

He then goes on to describe a slave caravan, some 3,000 strong, in stomach-turning detail.

A group of slaves

Slavery had been a quite fundamental element in local African society for centuries: successful chiefs used slaves for construction and agricultural work, especially where labour was in short supply and they also acquired wealth through the trade, in the form of cloth, beads, guns, etc. Successful warrior chiefs were usually successful slave and ivory traders. In the densely populated Shire Highland region of what is now Malawi, it was estimated that 20,000 slaves were captured each year in the 1860's. (By creating a new market for ivory, it could be said that the ALC contributed to the slave trade rather than reducing it, with Arab traders impressing villagers in their ivory hunts.)

Stevenson investigated this trade, the areas and routes most affected, and the huge wastage resulting not only from deaths of slaves being driven to the coast, but also the depopulation of once thriving districts. The answer, as far as Stevenson was concerned, following Livingstone's precepts, was to develop legitimate trade to displace the commerce in humanity, which could only happen if markets could be developed and the indigenous population was able to get the goods of the country to those markets cheaply. Notwithstanding the undoubted horrors of the slave trade, the latter was an expedient justification for displacing the Arab traders by Scottish ones.

Livingstone himself believed in the creation of a cash crop economy dominated by European traders, who would buy ivory, cotton and other goods, thus avoiding the necessity for Africans to sell slaves for the guns, powder, and calico which they wanted. He was especially interested in the growing of cotton to bypass the slave-owning states of USA—whether these commercial activities were carried out by missions or private entrepreneurs to him was immaterial. He was also a great supporter of steam power in the form of steamboats, having seen their potential on the great waterways of North America.

James Stevenson

Stevenson clearly had his eye on the possibilities of utilising the system of lakes and river systems in East/Central Africa, including Lake Tanganyika, Lake Nyasa (now Malawi) and the Zambezi and Shire Rives, for relatively cheap transport of goods, and he had been able to show that a previous compass error had positioned the north end of Lake Nyasa much closer to the East African coast than was the case: importantly, his calculations (he was an accomplished mathematician) reduced the previously computed distance between the lakes by 120 miles. He railed against the tariffs imposed by the Portuguese for goods entering Mozambique, which was seen as a major deterrent to trade via their territories, while at the same time he was concerned at the increasing Arab influence through the slave trade. This was rampant in the area round Lake Nyasa and Lake Tanganyika and had reduced a relatively peaceful area at the time of Baron Carol Claus von Decken's pioneering travels in the 1860's to a state of almost constant warfare some 20 years later, which the aggressive Ngoni and other tribes exploited.

Like others, Stevenson envisaged the possibility of resolving some of these issues by developing trade and education – especially industrial training – through improved communications and Christian mission work. In particular he saw the potential of creating a great 'water route' linking the lakes to the Zambezi and the Indian Ocean covering a distance of almost 1,500 miles, with only 275 miles of overland transport—a hugely ambitious vision which was nothing less than the 'civilisation' of central Africa through commerce and the church. At the same time Stevenson recognised the need to use force to suppress Arab activities, with gunboats on the lakes, and he even proposed putting 1,000 rifles in the hands of loyal local tribesmen ostensibly for 'defensive' purposes – directly at odds with the general policy of the missions to ban trade in arms (and alcohol), even though the Portuguese were already heavily involved in this trade.

Stevenson saw the prospect of developing modern systems of agricultural and cash crops, such as rubber, gum copal, cotton, sugar, coffee, and tobacco through a series of trading stations at approximately 70 mile intervals from the coast to the lakes and even westwards into the Congo. (He went as far as to include the Nile and the Congo in his prospectus to embrace over 10,000 miles of waterway to be served mainly by steamships covering a trading area of 6 million square miles.) In the event, he and his business colleagues quickly learnt that this production could not be effected rapidly and that any immediate returns could only come from ivory, where they would be in direct competition with the Arab traders and hunters, who used slaves to transport the ivory to the coast. (The extent of this use may have been exaggerated for purposes of anti-slavery propaganda.) The ALC agents in Nyasaland[1] found themselves under constant

---

[1]   Although this name did not come into official use until 1907, it is used here for convenience.

pressure to provide ivory, and were obliged to employ European sport hunters for this purpose: by 1881 the company had effectively given up crop transportation in favour of ivory. In 1879 there was a complaint from one of the ALC directors, James Stephen, that the Moirs were not energetic enough in pursuing ivory and had paid too much (above the market rate in London) to Cecil Rhodes for what they had purchased. Ivory in fact steadily increased in value throughout the 1880s.

The means of converting this vision into practical action was through the Livingstonia Sub-Committee (formed at Queens Hall in Glasgow on 3 November 1874) of the Free Church of Scotland's Foreign Mission Committee. (The Free Church had been established after the great Disruption of 1843: one of their great strengths was foreign missions for which they had raised twice as much money as they had done under the previously undivided church). The Sub-Committee was established by the Rev. Dr. James Stewart, a missionary who had travelled independently to the Zambezi with Mary Livingstone to investigate the possibility of a mission in the area. He was present with Livingstone on the death and funeral of his wife, buried at Shupanga on the Zambezi. He was one of the first to suggest that commercial outlets should be associated with the missions, and was supported by his brother-in-law, John Stephen, the son of a wealthy shipowner, James White of Overtoun who had a chemical empire, James Young who developed the commercial extraction and use of paraffin, and James Stevenson – all of them Scottish magnates who were prepared to dig into their own pockets for the cause of African development.

Area (inner box) of 600 million square miles which Stevenson considered could be opened up to waterway trade

In the mid-1870s there was significant opposition to the mission becoming involved with trade, but also Stevenson argued that the church should 'openly countenance and in many ways cooperate with Christian men engaged in honourable commerce.' He considered that missions such as Livingstonia, first established at the south end of Lake Nyasa, were only one means of bringing east and central Africa into the world economy, but that this could not happen without a reduction in transport costs to provide an incentive for potential local agricultural producers. It was the Livingstonia Committee which master-minded the very considerable feat of getting the first screw steamboat, the *Ilala* on to Lake Nyasa in 1875 under the leadership of Lieut. E.D. Young R.N. which required porterage by 700 natives of each individual plate around the 50 miles of cataracts on the Shire River, to be re-assembled above the falls.

A first attempt to establish a trade route into the interior, stimulated by the high Portuguese tariffs on the Zambezi, was that of the Scottish shipowner Sir William Mackinnon—a member of the Livingstonia Committee—and the philanthropist Sir Fowell Buxton, supported by Stevenson, who envisaged a road from the coast to the lakes, to be complemented by one between them. Mackinnon was committed to the notion, promoted by King Leopold of the Belgians, of a great network of roads across the centre of Africa, linked by waterways and trading stations. This was very much part of the grand imperial dream of linking territories with British interests, by road, rail, telegraph line and steamboat – in this case, the British India steamship line owned by Mackinnon, serving ports in east and southern Africa. A decisive development in communications was the completion of the Suez Canal in 1869 which opened up the continent of Africa via the east coast and the regular monthly mail run which Mackinnon had established.

Mackinnon and Buxton tried to circumvent the Portuguese duties by building a road overland from Dar-es-Salaam on the East African coast to Lake Nyasa in 1877, an alternative to the traditional northern route from Bagamoyo to Ujiji on Lake Tanganyika which was plagued by rapacious tribal chiefs demanding increasingly expensive gifts for rights of passage. Two volunteers on this project were the Edinburgh brothers, John and Frederick Moir, (sons of Dr. John Moir, another member of the Livingstonia Committee) who were to feature prominently as managers of the trading company subsequently established on Lake Nyasa. The road was an expensive failure, undermined partly by a reduction in Portuguese tariffs on Zambezi trade and the inability of Mackinnon to secure trading concessions from the Sultan of Zanzibar. However, in the opinion of the well-informed British Consul at Zanzibar, John Kirk, the project was also badly managed, with inferior supervisors, and problems of drunkenness and dishonesty. (the Moirs for example had very difficult relations with Mayes, the English Sergeant of Engineers). In the event only some 70 miles of the so-called 'Mackinnon Road' was constructed through the feared malarial coastal belt, infested with tsetse fly, and precluding the use of draft animals, but some comfort was taken from the increasing use of the road and the making of side roads by local villagers.

The company which Stevenson was instrumental in establishing in 1874 was originally named the Livingstonia Central African Trading Company until its change to the African Lakes Company in 1878, which still operates under the name of the African Lakes Corporation today. There were a number of British trading companies in Africa at this time, particularly on the west coast, many of these started by Scots, but the Livingstonia company was unique. Unusually among such trading companies, and because of its avowedly philanthropic purposes, it was much more in the public eye. Its prospectus was drafted by Stevenson, with a subscribed capital in 1878 of £12,000 but its distinguishing mark was its Christian ethos and direct links with the missionary endeavour on Lake Nyasa, which provided its main market. But this also meant that it was neither 'fish nor fowl': neither a straightforward commercial concern with an overriding objective to be profitable, nor a strictly Christian institution with a philanthropic motive. The company was plagued by lack of experienced staff: in McEwan's time there were on average 20 Europeans, but sickness and absences greatly reduced the company's effectiveness.

The company became embroiled in the issue of slavery, and for the first time in this region, introduced wage labour relations into what had been a largely subsistence economy. Together with its under-capitalisation and muddled management, this led to a confusion of objectives and poor administration. It was never a commercial success and seemed to stumble from one crisis to another. Despite this, it had political aspirations, and was disastrously drawn into violent conflict with the Arab slavers, which brought it close to ruin in the late 1880s. Later, it was to be sidelined by the British administration when it attempted to secure a wider sphere of influence and trade monopoly by highly dubious treaties signed with local chiefs. Equally seriously, and against all its principles, it was accused of trading in arms and gunpowder. The main complaint of the missions however was not only its poor and irregular service, but the high prices charged for both goods and particularly transport of these, notably for the Church of Scotland mission at Blantyre. However it was on the basis of its general incompetence that, in a memorandum to the Foreign Office, the mission opposed the ALC's subsequent claim to the administration of nothing less than the whole of Nyasaland!

Joseph Thomson was later to give his opinion: 'A more rotten commercial concern which contrives to make a big noise and cackle in the world I have never seen' claiming that it was entirely made up of good intentions, but completely failed to carry these out. And yet, Dr. Robert Laws, the most famous head of the Livingstonia Mission in its early years, and which had good cause to criticise the company, said of its managers (the Moir brothers) 'They established a standard of commercial relationship and trust which has been of the utmost importance to Nyasaland – commercial adventurers arriving later, found that they could not do as they liked, but had to conform to the standard of justice already existing.' It is interesting that this statement says nothing about their efficiency, on which the young William McEwan was to comment frequently in his diary.

Part of the problem lay in the long lines of communication: the managing committee in Glasgow held the purse strings, but none of their members had first hand experience of African conditions, while communications between Glasgow and Nyasaland would often take many weeks to be received at either end. Even within Nyasaland itself there were formidable obstacles to communications between the mission stations and the vessels. A mechanical breakdown involved the ordering and shipment of parts from Britain, and there were frequent changes in staff: the artisans, who could be transferred between the mission and the trading company, were recruited in Scotland and were expected to give up prospects of career advancement, and to work for a pittance (about £60 per annum) under the uncomfortable and dangerous conditions of a highly unsettled African territory where premature death from disease was accepted. They were expected also to be of Christian convictions, of good moral character, and where necessary to participate in mission activity, even preaching on occasion.

Not all of them measured up to these demanding criteria – some were of narrow outlook and limited education and background, while others had to be repatriated because of their conduct. The most serious incident occurred just before McEwan's arrival in the country, when an artisan called Fenwick, working for the Blantyre Mission of the Church of Scotland, shot an important chief, Chipatulo, on the lower Shire, and was himself killed by the tribesmen, resulting in an uprising which threatened the whole missionary and trading enterprise when the *Ilala* was sunk at anchor and part of the *Good News* awaiting transhipment for the London Missionary Society (LMS) was destroyed. McEwan was fortunate in having as his assistant Donald Munro who not only had road construction experience under the civil engineer, James Stewart, but seems to have been of sterling character and adaptable personality.

Boats were the lifeblood of communications between the missions and the trading stations, as well as conveying goods to larger steamships lying off the mouth of the Zambezi. During McEwan's time, there were two in particular which provided these services, i.e. the *Ilala* and the *Lady Nyassa*. The *Ilala*, named after the place where Livingstone died, was bought by Stevenson for the Free Church, and built by Messrs Yarrow and Headley in 1875. Some 48 feet long, it had a steel hull, made of plates fastened by bolts – each plate weighing 50 pounds. She drew only 3 feet of water, driven by a single propeller. Its first voyage, after assembly at the mouth of the Zambezi, was up the Shire River on 10 August 1875. After 5 days travel it had to be disassembled for porterage round the Murchison Falls and reassembled on the Zambezi at Matope. It was the first steam vessel to sail on the upper Shire and Lake Nyasa. The *Lady Nyassa* which McEwan refers to, was the second boat of that name, and was assembled in 1878 by the Moir brothers at Quelimane at the mouth of the Zambezi.

Transport of steamer sections

A flat-bottomed paddle steamer, it was 60 feet long by twelve feet broad, drawing 15 inches of water. For many years this vessel ran a fortnightly service from Maruru to Katunga's. (By the end of the nineteenth century there were not less than 17 steamers on the rivers and lake.)

Engineers and seamen from Scotland were hired to pilot and maintain these vessels, but although the latter were adequate for the Mission's purposes in its pioneering days, they were quite unsuited to the requirements of a commercial trading company with high commercial ambitions. The condition of the Shire and Zambezi Rivers combined with the smallness and shallow draft of both vessels meant that they had very limited capacity and could only profitably carry high value goods. There were frequent breakdowns, the *Ilala* could not maintain steam, and staff complained about the very poor living conditions aboard both vessels. The necessary use of porters between the Shire Highlands and the river further increased costs.

The route from the Indian Ocean to Lake Nyasa was first seriously explored by a Royal Geographical Society Expedition in 1879 initially led by the Edinburgh cartographer Keith Johnston prior to his premature death at Behobeho, near the Rufiji River. Following his death, his 21 year-old deputy, Joseph Thomson not only succeeded in reaching Lake Nyasa, but also surveyed a route north to the southern end of Lake Tanganyika, where, as he dramatically described above, he had a completely unexpected encounter at Pambete at the southern end of that lake, with another Scot, James Stewart, (cousin to the Rev. Dr. James Stewart referred to above) who was on a similar reconnaissance on behalf of the Livingstonia Mission.

Stewart, a key figure in both the physical development of that mission and the construction of the Stevenson Road, had come to Nyasaland in 1876, then aged 32, on leave from his work as a qualified Army civil engineer on the Sirkhind Canal in India. He was at a cross-roads in his career, and had been invited by his cousin to consider whether he should become involved with the Livingstonia Mission. However his first significant contribution, as a volunteer, was in the laying out of the physical infrastructure of Blantyre, the Church of Scotland's main mission in Nyasaland and which was to become the nucleus of the modern city of that name. Equally important, through his disciplined organisation and leadership, was the boost that he gave to the morale of that mission at a time when it was in serious danger of collapse.

He decided to throw in his lot with the missionaries, and in 1879 was appointed officially to the Livingstonia Mission. In 1878 and 1879, he made two important exploratory journeys to the north of the country. The first of these was with Dr. Robert Laws and William Koyi, and resulted in the establishment of two new mission stations, one of which was Bandawe on the lake shore, referred to frequently in the following diaries. The second was with John Moir of the ALC who before Stewart met Joseph Thomson at the southern end of Lake Tanganyika, had to return south with an infected foot. Stewart was a meticulous observer, as his expedition diaries edited by Dr. Jack Thompson show, and his maps were subsequently published in the Proceedings of the Royal Geographical Society, of which he was elected a Fellow. In 1880, he returned to Scotland and argued the case for the construction of a road between Lake Nyasa and Lake Tanganyika, strongly supported by James Stevenson. Stevenson was committed to the road between the lakes, and was determined to see it through. Following the Livingstonia Committee's refusal to provide financial support for this, it was Stevenson who personally subscribed the funds—then the not inconsiderable sum of £4,000—to employ Stewart as the first surveyor and engineer on this road in the summer of 1881 with his assistant, Donald Munro.

An important consideration was to persuade the London Missionary Society (LMS) which was under severe financial difficulties, to substitute its previous northern supply route to its mission station on Lake Tanganyika via Arab-dominated Ujiji, by the southern Livingstonia route via the Zambezi and Lake Nyasa, mainly in order to defray costs. After convoluted negotiations and not a little pressure from the main proponents of the Lake Nyasa route, (i.e. Stevenson and Stewart) the LMS agreed, partly because of the failure of their trial with ox-waggons along the traditional route to Ujiji, the deaths of their missionaries en route, and the problem of both costs and insecurity (one missionary had been brutally murdered). The offer from Stevenson of £4,000 to the LMS, the Livingstonia Mission, and the Livingstonia Trading Company, to meet the cost of constructing the road between the lakes, provided that the LMS established a station on the road, was on the basis that the Free Church did likewise, and that the trading company extended its commercial operations as far as Lake Tanganyika.

The Free Church mission station, under the Rev. J. Alexander Bain, was to be at Mweniwanda, which features prominently in both diaries, a distance of about 60 miles from Karonga, the company's main store in the north, and base for work on the road, with a further 190 miles to Lake Tanganyika. Crucially, there was agreement to ship the LMS steamer the *Good News* almost a thousand miles via the Nyasa route, thus guaranteeing an income to the Livingstonia trading company at a critical time in their moves to supplant the Arabs at the north end of Lake Nyasa. The road was to end at the LMS mission station at Niumkorlo on Lake Tanganyika. All of this Stevenson felt was essential to consolidate his dream of securing a viable trade route (not least for ivory) and Scottish paramountcy throughout the length of Nyasaland, but clearly to influence the commercial development along Lake Tanganyika, with the ultimate aim of displacing the Arabs, especially from the lucrative ivory trade. (Karonga was selected as a trading station in 1879 mainly to exploit the large herds of elephants which inhabited the marshes to the north of the Songwe River). There was considerable trade done with the big Arab traders for ivory at Karonga prior to McEwan's arrival, mainly by the ALC agent, Monteith Fotheringham.

F. Moir describes the route:

> '... the ascent to the great inland tableland began ... The next 50 miles were very difficult, being steep and also so far from water ... The steepest ascents were overcome by zigzags cut in the hillside, while rocks and boulders were

removed to secure a good passage ... Prospecting over these difficult hills to select the best contours was heavy work ... turning up of soil in swamps and valleys was especially trying ... outdoor work on the dry treeless plain is very trying during the day; mosquitoes, moths and flying ants are very annoying at night, while scorpions and snakes have also to be guarded against. There were many lions and hyenas...'

In fact, above the North Rukuru River, in places the road had to be cut into the hillside to a depth of up to 15 feet because of the contours, and rocks of several tons in weight were displaced in the process. Much of this initial section had been constructed by Stewart and Munro for 26 out of the 55 miles between Karonga and Mweniwanda before McEwan's arrival.

Professor Henry Drummond, a director of the ALC who had been sent by Stevenson to conduct a scientific survey of the country around the Stevenson Road wrote in his *Tropical Africa*:

'Forty-six miles of that road—probably the only thing of its kind in Central Africa have already been made entirely by native labour, and the work could not have been better done had it been executed by English navvies. I have watched by day a party of seventy natives working on a cutting upon that road. Till three or four years ago, none of them had ever looked upon a white man; nor till a few months previously had one of them seen a spade, a pickaxe or a crowbar. Yet these savages handled their tools to such purpose that, with only a single European superintendent, they have made a road, full of difficult cuttings and gradients, which would not disgrace a railway contractor at home. The workmen keep regular hours – six in the morning till five at night, with a rest at mid-day – work steadily, continuously, willingly, and above all merrily ... the only bribe for all this work is a yard or two of calico per week per man.'

Perhaps it should be mentioned that this somewhat rosy picture may have been penned for Stevenson's eyes, he being the sponsor of the work. Both Munro and McEwan refer to the difficulty in some districts in recruiting men, either as guides for his survey work, or for labour on the road. In May 1881 Stewart left with two artisans Ross and Munro to start work on the road and to establish new station at Chirenje near Mweniwanda's village about 50 miles inland of the lake. Stewart died in August 1883 before Rev. J. H. Bain, could take up post there. It is perhaps ironic that when Dr. Laws, then the head of the Livingstonia Mission, was showing Stewart the country after the latter's arrival, he indicated several graves of other Europeans, Stewart said 'This is a queer sort of country where the only things you have to show me are graves' to which Laws replied 'They are the milestones of Christianity, marking its advance into the interior.' Another distinguished traveller in the area at this time, Prof. Henry Drummond, after a relatively short period in the country, stated 'I have been in an atmosphere of death all the time' and according to his biographer, was permanently changed by his experience.[2]

A considerable problem was road maintenance – Stewart obtained agreement that the ALC should make a contribution of £50-100 per annum for its upkeep, but they could charge dues on use of the road to offset this. By the time McEwan arrived, a relatively short time after Stewart's death, the work he had done was being encroached on by the surrounding bush. There was serious discussion in Glasgow about the prospects of bringing over Indian elephants to help train African elephants (a proposal that had been mooted elsewhere to overcome African transport problems) as much for their ability to keep the track clear as for transport. It proved to be a quite impracticable suggestion: the experience of a Belgian expedition in 1879 attempting to use Indian elephants ended in disaster. Until the use of the combustion engine in the 20th century, circumventing the problem of draft animals afflicted by tsetse, head porterage by *tenga-tenga* was the most efficient form of transport, requiring minimal track clearance – wheeled vehicles involved road construction of a quite different order.

Nyasaland as it was known at this time, (although it was not officially recognised by that name until 1907) and now Malawi, is a country of considerable contrasts. By far the greatest extent of this long narrow territory – about 900 km long, or about the length of Britain – is occupied by Lake Nyasa (Malawi) lying between Tanganyika to the north, Mozambique (or Portuguese East Africa until the mid 20th century) to the east, and modern Zambia (formerly Northern Rhodesia) to the west. The lake, measuring 570 km in length and ranging from 16 to 80 km in width, is Africa's third, and the world's twelfth largest lake lying at approximately 450m above sea level along the line of the great Rift Valley. The highest mountain is Mulanje at 3002 metres, but to the west of the lake there are extensive plateaux averaging 900 to 1200 metres with the Dedza, Viphya, and Nyika plateaux reaching heights of 1500 to 2400 metres.

In a country of such variation in altitude there are corresponding differences in local climate and vegetation, influenced by the proximity of the lake. During the hottest months, from October onwards, the Rift Valley around the lake-shores can experience temperatures in excess of 38 degrees, while frost is common at the higher altitudes in the dry season between May and August. The rainy season is from November to April with annual falls varying between 60 and 300 cm, largely dependent on altitude and position. The vegetation is both

---

[2] See Smith, G. A , (1899) *The Life of Henry Drummond*, p. 211.

tropical and sub-tropical, but large areas are occupied by wooded grassland and open savannah, dominated by *Brachystegia* tree species with some extensive marshlands round the lake.

Although much of the country is unsuitable for cash crops, the central region and the Shire Highlands in the south are relatively fertile and can support large and varied crops of tobacco, tea, sugar, groundnuts, rice, cotton, coffee, and maize, while in the north, maize, tea, rice and rubber are grown. In the 1880s, on the more fertile alluvial soils around the lakeshore, native gardens supported cassava, sweet potatoes, millet, groundnuts, beans, pumpkins, bananas and plantains, while there was active iron smelting and much local trading here and elsewhere. Cattle were raised in tsetse-free areas, but generally sheep and goats were far commoner. Nyasaland was connected to the wider world by the time the British came by extensive trade from the coast right through to Katanga.

Karonga near the lake was a main base of operations for both the mission and the ALC, but the surrounding alluvial flatlands, which elsewhere can be up to 10 miles in width, give way rapidly to steep hills to the north and west, making for difficult travel. Soon after entering the hills, there are two large rivers to cross, the North Rukuru and the Mwesha, which although easily crossable in the dry season become raging torrents in the wet. After this stony and rocky ground predominates with some steep rocky climbs before the River Lufira is crossed. About 50 miles from Karonga the hill summits are reached and then the station at Mweniwanda[3] (Maliwanda) which was an important base for McEwan's work, and situated in a great amphitheatre of hills, dominated by the great broken massif of the Misuku Hills to the north east, rising to over 2000m. From here it would be a 2-3 week journey on foot to the southern shores of Lake Tanganyika, mainly over the rolling ridges of the open plateau.

Of the larger fauna, this description of an encounter by Fred Moir of the ALC is indicative:

'... on our return in the dinghy, as we were crossing the river to avoid a herd of hippos on ahead, a big bull from another herd on the opposite side made for us. We expected him to rise near, when he would have received the contents of our rifles. But no; the brute seized the bottom of the boat with his teeth, and gave it such a heave that I was shot over Stewart's head and plunged into the water, rifle in hand, revolver, heavy cartridges, and usual hunting accessories in my belt, and wearing coat, heavy walking boots, etc. The rifle was consigned to the bottom, and I struck out shorewards. The hippo crunched the boat three or four times, till Stewart thought it best to abandon it and follow, throwing off coat

---

[3]   As with other place names, the spelling is variable in the diaries Mweniwanda, Mwiniwanda, Maliwanda, etc.

and encumbrances. The blacks took to the water at once, and, not being troubled with clothes, arrived first. When, after a long swim I reached within six yards of the bank, I sank overweighted; but Stewart was now close behind me, and, taking my hand, guided me ashore as I swam underwater. My strength only sufficed to get one knee on the bank, and I fell exhausted. We were all the more thankful for our escape as the river abounds with crocodiles......with only one revolver among us, we had to retreat before a herd of buffaloes and camp out without food in a district with plenty of lions and mosquitoes....though the fear of the lions kept us watchful, the mosquitoes were the more active tormentors.'

(Moir records that previously there were a number of hippopotami in the Zambezi, but by 1885, there were few, but still plenty of crocodiles.) The area also supported a variety of antelope species and occasional troops of zebra. Lions were numerous locally, and leopard, jackals and hyena were common.

While (apart from the notorious massacre of African road workers in Stewart's time) neither Munro or McEwan were themselves involved in large scale confrontation with local Africans, in 1883 there was a potentially disastrous uprising against the Portuguese, which involved other Europeans, including ALC staff. At Chironji the natives massacred the Portuguese garrison, and it was only a mixed European force of 15 together with 90 natives led by Fred Moir which saved the day and the lives of those who had taken refuge in the ALC station at Mopea.

The Diaries

There are certain common features which come through from both of these diaries, albeit written by quite different personalities in quite distinctive styles. Sometimes Munro and McEwan were working together – and there is no suggestion that their relationship, even under very difficult circumstances, was other than amicable – and not infrequently, they were on their own i.e. without another white companion. However, they had from time to time the company of compatriots, for there never was a region of Africa more replete with Scots, whether missionaries, administrators, traders, or engineers, most if not all answering Livingstone's call. Prof. Drummond referred to above described the 'unutterable loneliness' which could afflict solitary travellers in Africa, recommending that two should always travel together. Apart from companionship, this was essential if they required nursing in time of sickness. Munro, who spent much longer in the continent than McEwan, and was often apart from his supervisor, James Stewart, particularly mentions this loneliness and his desire for European company. (The writer Jonathan Falla claimed that his Sudanese diaries were both a partial antidote to loneliness. 'Someone to talk to', and a way of making sense of his experiences – in effect addressing a letter to himself.)

This sense of isolation, and need for news of the familiar, is reflected in the sometimes desperate desire for mail from home, even if it contained nothing more than domestic trivia, which in itself might have been reassuring to those inhabiting an environment and culture which at times could hardly have seemed more alien and often frightening. Nothing seemed to have incensed the diarists more – especially McEwan – than the casual treatment of mail and its delayed delivery. That apart, it is difficult in these days of instant electronic and telephone communication, to appreciate the problems of relying almost entirely on the written word, not only for news, but even for urgent relaying of instructions between stations and Britain.

Both diarists make reference to the same problems – of enforced idleness while awaiting transport or men, of steamer delays, shortage of food, desertion of workers, chronic pilfering of stores, difficulty of recruitment of guides and porters, and the venality of truculent chiefs, not to mention what Munro in particular regarded as their dishonesty and deceitfulness. On top of this there was predation on stock and humans by carnivorous animals. Any one of these challenges could be surmounted, but their accumulation, especially when the

Europeans were on their own, could become unbearable. However, the 'straw which could break the camel's back' was tropical illness.

The issue of debilitating disease dominated all those who lived in central Africa at this time, affecting Africans and Europeans alike, although local people did seem to develop some immunity. Both diaries describe a catalogue of fevers and dysentery which could strike at any moment. There were no effective prophylactics against malaria, whose carrier, the *Anopheles* mosquito, had not been identified, although large doses of quinine could reduce the symptoms. Nor was there any appreciation of the need for total rest and rehydration in the case of dysentery, which could otherwise prove fatal, as it did in the case of Keith Johnston, the leader of the expedition to Lake Nyasa which Joseph Thomson successfully completed.

Even during his last illness, McEwan bathed in the lake waters, with no knowledge at that time of the threat of bilharzia, the very serious water-borne disease transmitted by a freshwater snail at the lake margins. Prof. Drummond who visited Nyasaland in Munro's time, refers to the desirability of Europeans having a travelling companion, so that each could nurse the other in turn – precisely the situation which McEwan and Munro found themselves in throughout their time together. More often than not, those who were ill did not know the nature of their condition, let alone its treatment, while identifiable afflictions such as toothache could prostrate victims without professional attention or effective analgesics.

Both men make references to the dispositions of their fellow workers, and McEwan in particular is scathing about the competence of the ALC, although this may be partly due to his own youthful inexperience and lack of appreciation of the management problems involved. There is no lack of comment on the failings of others, even among the missionaries, which McEwan somewhat righteously criticises, unaware that in the process, he is guilty of the same sin. For his part, Munro typically reserves his most scathing comments for those who do not attend to their practical duty, to ensure for example, that his tools in store are not destroyed by white ants.

All of these problems could either be a source of friction between the pioneers, given their intimate proximity in the bush, or conversely, because of their mutual dependence, contribute to their bonding and concern for each other's welfare, which seems to have been the case with the two Scots, at least from the record of their private diaries. There is good reason to suppose that having witnessed the death of his first mentor, James Stewart, the demise of McEwan after a relatively short period in the country, coupled with his own illnesses, may well have been the final psychological straw as far as Munro was concerned when he agreed to leave the country in 1885.

Donald Munro was born at Castleton, near Lochgilphead in Argyll, the son of a boat-builder, and followed in his father's footsteps, taking his training as a boat-builder and joiner at the famous Govan shipyard on the Clyde. He was one of six children, two of his brothers eventually settling in Australia. The rural community he came from was a close knit one, and relatively remote in the latter half of the 19th century, situated on the shores of Loch Fyne, with a strong sea-faring and fishing tradition. All the indications are that Munro was a tough, adaptable, and self-reliant young man with the uncomplicated and robust Christian faith characteristic of that background. At Govan, he was a member of the Free St. Mary's Church which appears to have had a particularly important association with missions, supporting a number of artisans who worked for the Livingstonia Mission. (It was the workers of this church who presented Munro with a hand made travelling desk prior to his departure for Africa at the age of 23.) From the church reports however, his family would not have been unaware that a quarter of the young men who went to central Africa died before their early thirties.

William O. McEwan (the 'O' stands intriguingly for 'Ottowa') born in 1863, came from a middle-class Glasgow family, his father James McEwan being a manufacturer of fancy lady's costumes who died when William was 5 years old. Not surprisingly he was very close to his widowed mother Margaret. It appears that he may have had three brothers, Robert, James and John and two sisters, Mary and Jeannie, though this is only inferred from references in his diary. The family must have been reasonably well established to be able to afford civil engineering training for William, and the evidence of his diary indicates a sound Scottish education, with a considerable background in reading at an early age. There is no indication that the family had any specific overseas connections, but like so many other young men of his time, William had a strong attachment to his church, the Free Church of Scotland, and a certain missionary zeal. No other personal background has been uncovered regarding William or his family.

Donald Munro's diary, commencing 10th May 1881, is the usual foolscap bound volume written in a large hand, with entries for each day. It is currently held by his great granddaughter, and unlike Munro's, is accompanied by a number of coloured sketches executed by himself. Where McEwan's notes are discursive, Munro is usually brief and to the point, concentrating on practical matters. He certainly cannot be accused of undue introspection, and while this is admirable in a man of action, it provides less material for revealing his emotions and psychology. One result is that there is a disparity in the reflections of this editor on the character and personality of the two men respectively.

As Munro is responsible for ensuring food supplies, it is perhaps not surprising that his diary has frequent references to hunting not only for the pot, but also for ivory and indeed pure sport. Some of the descriptions of the latter do not appear particularly 'sporting' in the many descriptions of wounding animals which are not followed up and the usual disregard for wildlife slaughter which was common enough at the time. (Conversely McEwan seems to have no interest in gamesport or the acquisition of hunting trophies.)

Like McEwan, Munro demonstrates his Christian faith without sermonising: all associated with the missions appear to have been at least encouraged to lead prayer meetings or prosetylise in the districts while at mission stations, and to use every opportunity for conveying their faith to local people. (Despite this, or perhaps because of it, both men hint at their doubts as to the effectiveness of the missionaries.) For this, they required to be reasonably proficient in Chinyanja, in which Munro had a head start on McEwan, to the extent that he was frequently the spokesman for the younger engineer at meetings with chiefs and in negotiating with the work force. That apart, there is no doubt that committed artisans such as Munro, with their manual skills and ability to turn their hand to a wide range of practical tasks using any available materials, were worth their weight in gold: the road construction work for example was largely carried out with nothing more than hoes, crowbars, and axes.

The diary of William McEwan like Munro's, is contained in a single foolscap folio currently in the keeping of the Royal Scottish Geographical Society. (RSGS) It was given to the Society by the United Society for Christian Literature in 1942, together with an extract from an earlier diary and some correspondence with the renowned Victorian biologist Thomas H. Huxley. Because of their interest, these last items are reproduced in Appendix 2. They provide an insight into the motivation and character of the 20-year old Scots civil engineer, who like so many others, was inspired from an early age by the example of David Livingstone to dedicate his life to African development.

Thus he writes somewhat ingenuously to Professor Huxley (then H.M. Inspector of Fisheries) seeking advice on how best to train himself for this task: McEwan's detailed account of his interview with Huxley may well be unique. Certainly he came away impressed by both the man and his eminently practical advice, recommending a scientific government-sponsored course at Kensington, although it is not known whether McEwan took this up. Given the 2-3 year period required however, and the date of his departure for Africa, this is most unlikely. (In his diary he records his inadequacy to detail scientific phenomena and his desire to undertake further training in this field before considering a return to Africa.) The establishment at South Kensington which Professor Huxley was associated with is likely to be the British Natural History Museum although there is also a reference to Kew, perhaps for some practical outdoor aspects of the course.

It is interesting to note some of Huxley's comments, for example, on the ephemeral results of most explorers' discoveries, notwithstanding the temporary fame which they might gain. This had been a contentious issue for some time in the debates of the Royal Geographical Society i.e. whether expeditions should now eschew 'spectacular' exploration in favour of more systematic scientific survey. (McEwan saw his work in the field of exploration.) Huxley is equally forthright in his opinion on the work of the missions. Despite his own Christian faith, McEwan in his diary was to give vent to his own critical comments on the value of mission work as it was carried out at that time in Nyasaland, and it is doubtful if he would have described himself as a missionary as was done in the obituary of the *Free Church Monthly*, which seemed anxious to claim another martyr.

What is known is that he gained the Cuthbert Peek prize in geology and astronomy awarded by the Royal Geographical Society on one of their courses for intending travellers: clearly he was an able and diligent student, imbued with great determination and earnestness. It is also obvious from this early entry in his diary that he is given to considerable self-examination and sense of purpose at a relatively early stage in his life. His concern at his possible lack of perseverance for the task he has set himself certainly seems misplaced. At the same time, these notes on his interview with the renowned Professor are an indication of his verbosity in writing which is a feature of his African diary.

McEwan's diary indicates that he spent some time in Natal, before pro-ceeding north to Quelimane, in the Portuguese-administered territory of Mozambique *en route* to take up his position with the ALC as engineer in charge of building the Stevenson Road. McEwan was a punctilious diarist and recorded his daily life and travels in great – and sometimes tedious – detail virtually up to the month of his premature death at the age of 21 on 25 May 1885, and almost exactly two years after his interview with Huxley. Abstracts from the early section of that diary were published in the *Geographical Magazine* (the journal of the RSGS) by the Honorary Editor, John F. Stewart, 1942. This is in two parts in 1942, but an intended third part does not seem to have been published.

McEwan arrived at Quelimane, on the coast, on 21st April 1884, and his diary provides an intimate picture of the town and its various inhabitants at this time. As a civil engineer, he is obviously interested in its buildings and their construction, the wharves, drainage systems, etc. He describes the construction of the *machila,* the African equivalent of the sedan chair, which was the main means of transport, the appearance of the natives, and the social life of the community (which as a strict Free Church Presbyterian he does not approve of). His comments on the Portuguese as colonists and native Africans would nowadays be regarded as racist, but were comparatively mild for their time. He is clearly imbued with the notion that the British are superior empire builders, though it is interesting to note, as a Scot, (who were dominant in Nyasaland at this time) his conventional use of 'English' to represent all Britons.

McEwan departed up the Zambezi on the first leg of his journey northwards to Lake Nyasa and gives a very interesting description not only of the first native village of Maruru which he encounters, but also of the life and daily routine of a trading station of the ALC which it purchased in 1882 – and his first veiled criticism of the operation of the latter. His descriptions of the landscape and conditions indicate accurate observation, even if his comment on the source of malaria – as a 'miasma' which hung on the low ground in the early morning – was no more than the current misapprehension of this lethal disease. One of the most interesting comments is his discussion on the rights and wrongs of the hypothetical purchase of a slave boy by a European conveniently overlooking, in his comparison with registries of servants in Britain at the time, the means by which the slave might have been acquired in the first place and the cruelties involved.

The approach which has been followed in both diaries is to select those passages which seem to convey best both the daily life of the pioneers and significant events, focussing on what seemed to the editor to be the more interesting comments, right up to the point where in nursing Munro who has contracted the dreaded blackwater fever, McEwan falls prey to the same disease, when his diary abruptly ends on May 8. McEwan was assiduous in writing up his diary, detailing everything from awakening each morning to the time of retiring at night, not excluding (it seems) every meal he ate, so that the abstracts have necessarily been very selective. However, unlike the original published parts, the abstracts are set within the context of the operations of the ALC and the general situation in which the diarists found themselves, with explanatory notes by this editor. McEwan was buried at Karonga on the shores of Lake Malawi, but after flooding, the gravestones were moved a little further inland, together with those of Stewart and Gowans. The diary records the constant battle with fevers – as with others in tropical Africa at this time, McEwan in particular suffered more days with sickness than good health – it is a constant theme of these diaries and other accounts of travellers along the unhealthy low-lying shores of the lakes.

What comes through from McEwan's writing are a number of aspects of his character and personality, with due allowance for his youth. No doubt in time his ingenuousness, almost naivete, would have become modified by experience and maturity, although he might also have retained that earnestness which is so marked in his diary. Both he and Munro certainly exemplified Henry Morton Stanley's observation that what marked out the Scots from others was their sense of duty, carried out under very demanding and often dangerous circumstances. He comes over as a very upright young man, anxious not only to fulfil his obligations, but also not to waste his time on unnecessary frivolities, but to continually seek opportunities for self-improvement (mainly through reading of serious works) and the development of his character. (Munro likewise read 'improving works' but as a practical man, seemed to concentrate on enhancing his mathematics.)

Unlike Munro (and other diarists in similar situations) McEwan is very forthcoming about his personal feelings and emotions, and the diary therefore provides an unusually intimate picture of what it must have been like for a very young pioneer, experiencing an exotic tropical environment and culture for the first time. Further, as the editor of the Scottish Geographical Magazine commented at the time of receiving the diary, it is difficult to imagine anyone in these more hectic days sitting down in a tent after a hard day's work in an unhealthy and enervating climate and, by the light of a candle, and in McEwan's case, entering in a private diary the details of every incident that occurred during the day, his experiences of the country, the climate, his helpers, native life and customs, and to illustrate the happenings by neat pen-and-ink sketches.

In his condemnation of others whom he considers lazy, inefficient or uncultured, McEwan could have been accused of a certain priggishness—indeed his comments on habits of other nationalities, notably the Portuguese in the previously published parts are both righteous and censorious. But there is nothing mean or devious in either of these two men, and there is in their dedication to their task and determination to overcome difficulties, a genuinely heroic and unselfish streak which is admirable. In many ways, they seem to have embodied the archetypal Victorian ideal of 'muscular Christianity' and 'manliness', but particularly in McEwan's case, with a touching devotion to his family at home. The remark by the Rev. Bain, that his men were much moved at his burial, as one of their favourites, rings true, and is very much of a piece with a character which was essentially open and caring.

What these young men were asked to do was nothing less than the construction of the most ambitious road project in Africa at that time, being given instructions from Stevenson who had no direct experience of African conditions. (McEwan was even asked on his way up to the north to survey the prospects for a future railway, merely as a sideline to his main work.) At the same time, it is clear from the diaries that they were provided with minimal equipment and technical support, so that they had to become very self-reliant. Only passing reference is made to the equipment carried, the instruments used and the techniques of surveying. If they had followed Thomson's advice in the RGS publication *Hints to Travellers* all their equipment would have been carried in watertight boxes of a size and shape to be comfortably carried on the shoulders or heads of porters, none of them weighing in excess of 50 pounds, to allow for the additional personal gear of their men. Thomson, after his salutary experience on his first expedition, strongly recommends that travellers should make themselves as comfortable as circumstances permitted, particularly in the matter of the size of tent, together with a folding table, chair, etc.

Sir John Kirk, in the same publication, detailed the survey instruments to include a 6 inch sextant, a mercurial or artificial horizon, a pocket chronometer, compasses, aneroid barometer, thermometers, etc. emphasising the need for particular care in protecting these often heavy instruments. (For this purpose, the boxes were to be brass-bound.) The accurate use of these required considerable skill and quite complex calculations. John Coles, instructor to the RGS, made it clear that this required a knowledge of trigonometry and practical astronomy, both involving specific training since 'it is scarcely possible to map the country ..., nor will (the traveller) be able to take full advantage of these *Hints*, as the greater part of the matters dealt with will be beyond his comprehension.'

Both diaries are assiduously written up, usually at the end of each day, sometimes when the writer was quite unwell. It is a reflection of the times that whereas other artisans are referred to by their surnames only, McEwan and Stewart are always designated by Munro 'Mr' as with other professionals, while conversely McEwan simply refers to 'Munro'. In these diaries it is not easy to track the various journeys up and down the lake and across the plateau, complicated by variable spelling of place names, while different authors use different spellings – no attempt has been made to correct these or make them consistent. For example, the use of the term Angoni (Ngoni) for a tribe is now antiquated. All references to Tanganyika refer to the lake, and more particularly its southern terminus, since at this time, the name Tanganyika was not yet applied to the country to the east. Italics have been used for the editor's own insertions. For readability, some of the longer passages have been broken up into paragraphs, and occasionally punctuation of Munro's diary has been altered. Munro's diary has occasional spelling mistakes which have been retained where the meaning is clear.

Abstracts from the Diary of Donald Munro

3 August - 31 December 1881 Massacre: A Baptism of Fire

Munro and his companions including James Stewart arrived at Zanzibar on June 26 1881 and were given a hearty welcome by Bishop Steere who conducted them round the new cathedral. By July 8, Munro and Stewart had arrived at Quilimane in Portuguese territory and started their journey up river. The following narrative is in Munro's words.

August 3 *(On the Shire River)*
The river seemed to be alive with hippopotamus ... I am sure we passed over a hundred during the day.

August 4
... When at dinner we saw 14 crocodiles on opposite bank. (of Shire)

August 5
When the big boat arrived they told us that one of the canoes met with a sad fate, as a hippo struck it and threw one of the men overboard. It then made for the Maggie, when Mr. Moir[4] and Mr. Stewart lodged a bullet each in his head, which I suppose put an end to all his troubles ...

August 9 *At Mandala Munro met an old companion, J M McIlwain, who had been with Munro at Free St. Mary's Church, Govan with a gift from that church.*

August 14 *First reference to fever.*

September 25 *(Bandawe)*
... While on the hill there were a number of children with small baskets busy catching the *kungu* fly. These flies pass along the lake in great clouds, so the natives make cakes of them. They are a little larger than the midge. ... I was much interested in the fashion of the natives which I thought was not to be envied. The women delight in wearing peleles (lip discs). They differ greatly that some have white stones, others red beads, and some have bits of lead, etc. these they wear in the upper lip. They vary in size from an eighth of an inch to two inches. And they clot the head with oil and red ochre. And their bodies get all smeared with it also – both sexes indulge in this nasty habit ...

---

[4]   The reference is to John Moir (c/f his brother Fred) general manager of the African Lakes Company.

Oct 7

... Reached a village belonging to Kandakera, so we encamped for the night. We were presented with a goat from the chief, four handkerchiefs were given in return, we got to our beds about nine, the three of us huddled in one tent.

Oct 8

Rose at six, had breakfast. The camp in a perfect uproar, through having so much *nyama* (beef)—*Stewart has shot a hippo on the previous day, and also some of the men rebelled against going any further, as they thought we were going to Tanganyika direct.*

Oct 12 *(Nyondo)*

... We had some amusement with the natives. We were showing them their own faces in a looking glass. Some were well pleased, others were horrified at their own ugly appearance ...

Oct 13

... got to Chiwinda at 4. pm We all felt very thankful to get to our journey's end. Making in seven days a distance of eighty six miles. After pitching our tent, Chiwinda[5] came and presented us with a tusk – he was well paid in return. After worship we got early to our beds.[6]

Oct 22

After starting the men to the house, Mr. Stewart started to line of a few miles of the road, as it will require to pass through this valley. Sent for the chief and accused him of deceiving me by promising to give some women to work and sending none. He went away a little displeased, and returned almost immediately afterwards with twelve women laden with grass. I also got twelve men to work. The greatest novelty they see in working for us was having their names called from a book. They do not believe in a day's work for a day's wages ...

Nov 20 Sabbath

We had worship in the morning, after which I started writing. At midday Mr. Stewart arrived all well, but bringing the sad tiding that fourteen of our men and eight of Chiwinda's were massacred on Thursday the 17th inst. The news caused great consternation amongst the villagers. We hoped however that it was not true ...

Nov 21

We could not get all our men to work as they wanted a day to mourn the loss of their friends ... Chiwinda was up today asking us to join him in war and punish the murderers. We declined, he went away very angry ...

---

[5] Place names frequently took the names of local tribal chiefs.

[6] This was the start of the road and for several weeks, Munro was engaged in building huts for a base station.

Nov 22

I had a visit of the chief today, he was in company with an Arab slaver who passed himself off as a chief from Malasaka ... I feel as if the villagers instigated by the slavers are on for some mischief. After committing myself to Him who is able to take care of me, I went to bed but could not sleep.

Nov 23

Rose about four, had a sleepless night ... when at dinner, the men came up to me in a breathless state, telling that they were put out of their *nsasa* (hut) by the chief, and that he, joined by another chief called Tambarara was coming to make war with me. I got all the guns in readiness in case of an attack, shortly afterwards word was sent that the chief did not want to make war. So I returned the word that I was indifferent whether or not, as there is nothing like independence amongst this people. At seven o'clock seven men arrived that were despatched by Mr. Moir bringing a letter with the sad tidings of as follows. 'Last night, that being November. 18 about 6, thirty four of the party that left Chiwinda to come here, arrived saying that all their companions had been killed in cold blood at Nyumbera's village ... they saw Malopa, one of the two who went to see the chief speared in the back, while the other had his head opened with a *nangwapi* (bill-hook) ... the rest scattered, three hid in the river, four made good their escape by running. They got to a village about three, where they rested being worn out. They were suddenly come on, and only one escaped. That being eleven of our men and eight of Chiwinda's massacred.' I felt thankful for the timely arrival of Mr. Moir's men, as I believe it prevented mischief during the night.

Dec 2

... I was instructed by a letter (from Mr. Stewart) to let Chiwinda know that there is a raid to be made on Nyumbera the following Wednesday. I delivered the message which was received with great enthusiasm, and he was to collect all the neighbouring chiefs to assist him. I was further told that the people were not to kill anybody unless it could not be avoided, but they were to catch all the cattle they could, as the idea was to rout him out of the valley ...

Dec 5

I have got everything about the house finished, so I intend doing no more until Mr. Stewart comes. About thirty men arrived from Maliwanda, all well armed.[7] Another chief called Tambarara had a good number of men. They had a war dance in the afternoon. It was a source of amusement for me to see them jumping about like wild beasts flashing their spears and firing their guns. I have all things in readiness for tomorrow.

---

[7]   Maliwanda, later more usually spelt as Mweniwanda, was an outpost mission and ALC store about 50 miles north west of Karonga on the Stevenson Road (see map).

Dec 6

This being the day they were to start for the valley I gave all the warriors a red badge for their heads that they might know one another ... I sent between seventy and eighty men for the valley. As I was instructed to get all things ready for emergency, so I began to pack all the goods.

Dec 11 *(Munro had met up with Stewart, Moir, and Fairley but had apparently lost Ross)*
... At 4.45 Ross did not arrive and he being first of the party, we felt anxious for him, we sent three men in search of him, we sent other two at 5. At 5.45 I started at took a lantern and two men. I went out to where he was last seen, a distance of four miles. I met all the other men turning, so I took them with me as it was very dark. While passing through a dense forest, a lion began to roar within a hundred and fifty yards of us and the men got very frightened and was for scattering and managed to keep them beside me ... other two lions began with their dreadful roaring only a little further away ... *(met up with Ross in camp at eight o'clock)*

Dec 12

... Ross gave me the following account of the war. They entered the valley on Wednesday morning 7 December. Found that the people had fled to the hills, taking all their cattle with them. They could see small groups here and there on the hills, but could easily scatter them by firing a shot in their direction. They burned between three and four hundred houses, they pursued the people for a day or two, but to no purpose. They got a few cattle sent to them, there were only two or three of Nyumbera's men killed. The people that were sent from here did not arrive in the valley till Thursday, when it was too late; I hope this may be a lesson to the people here that they cannot kill our men with impunity ... *Later, Munro was told that after the massacre one of their own men did a deal with a local chief which involved taking cattle in the name of the white men in return for a tusk which the scoundrel took to Quilimane for sale. Munro left Chiwinda on 13 December for Maliwanda.*

Dec 18 (Sabbath)

Rose at 5.45 got coffee and prepared for the journey. At 6.45 we got a start, the day fine for a march. We rest at a village at 9 where we had breakfast. We got underway again at 11 am. We stopped for dinner at two, after passing over a splendid part of the country. We started at 3.30. We passed an Arab village at 4.30, so we pushed on to get to Maliwanda, so we managed there at 7:30. We found Messrs. Stewart, Moir and Fairley all well. I felt rather tired after 26 miles of journeying. After worship we got to our beds.[8]

---

[8]   Under any circumstances, these distances covered through the African bush were remarkable, but his was a not atypical day.

Dec 25 *(Sabbath)*

Rose at 7 wished each other A Merry Christmas. After breakfast we had worship. Mr. Moir made a Christmas pudding of ufa (native meal) as we had nothing else, our stores being very low. It tasted very well. We had hymn singing in the evening.[9]

Dec 28

Rose and got the skin (zebra) stretched and cleaned. At 10 am we saw the *Ilala* coming ... Mr. Moir and Oftedahl arrived with the mails ... I received 17 letters and 9 newspapers, I had a light heart when I read all well at home ...[10]

Dec 31

I was writing some letters during the day, in the evening it was reported that a chief called Mosao and Kangoma was at Karonga on their way to make war with Malasaka.

---

[9] This after-dinner worship was not confined to missionaries *per se* and obviously boosted morale.

[10] Both Munro and McEwan refer frequently to the arrival of mail from home as a high point in their existence and their impatience to receive it.

January 1 – 31 December 1882 Ferocious Fauna: From Leopards to Lions.

Jan 1 (*Bandawe*)
Rose and wished Mr. Stewart a good new year ... I made a plum pudding for dinner. Mrs Laws was kind enough to send spices, etc. which made the pudding first class. We had a visit from the warriors that is on their way to Malasaka ...

Jan 2
... I gave the men their New Year by giving them a fowl each.[11]

Jan 3
I think the men that were here have started on their expedition against Malasaka. I got my blankets washed and had a headache and went to bed after dinner.

Jan 4
... started for Rombashi at 12.40 arrived there at 4.15 just in time to see Malasaka's people beating a retreat, they were crossing to the north side of the Mbashi, driving their cattle before them. Mr. Stewart said there would be about three thousand people that crossed the river this evening. It was a fine sight to see them and hear both cattle and people roaring as they fled.

Jan 8 (Sabbath) *At Bandawe*
... I then attended the native meeting, where I was glad to see Dr. Hannington, Mrs Hannington, and W. Koyi.[12] The meeting was addressed by Dr Laws and Koyi. There were a large attendance of natives.

Jan 14
... I killed a snake about 4 feet long and two and a half in diameter ...

February 6 *First reference to lessons in Chinyanja.*[13]

February 7
Getting the shop read up.[14] This being my 24th birthday. W Koyi arrived from the Angoni country, having three of the chiefs and about twenty of their followers.[15] The head chief

---

[11]   Here Munro is following traditional Scottish custom in celebrating New Year rather than Christmas.
[12]   William Koyi had been brought from the mission school at Lovedale in South Africa as a lay preacher and proved invaluable, not least for his ability to interpret local languages.
[13]   Although different tribes spoke their own language, the *lingua franca* of Nyasaland was Chinyanja.
[14]   Correctly spelt 'redd', the Scots word for 'cleaned up.'

that is down is called Chipatula who has done a great deal of mischief in this country. They have their hair pleated, like a forage cap. I was at the class in the evening. (*presumably Chinyanja*)

February 10

Felt rather seedy, after breakfast took bad with biliousness, I lay in bed most of the day, Ross also seedy. In the evening we had a magic lantern entertainment, it pleased the Angoni very much.

March 20 *At Bandawe*

... (Ross) told me that a few days before they arrived at Matope, an attack was made on Kalamba's village by the Maviti. They killed a number and took a good number prisoner. Old Kalamba was killed within a few yards of the house we have there. It is supposed that he would think himself safe if he got to the Englishman's house. But he met his death on his way to it. I got my letters at 5.30 – I had four and two papers. We were all invited to tea by Mrs Laws, which we all enjoyed.

April 2 (Sabbath)

At the native service. I had Capt. Gowans and Ross at dinner. I managed to give a fair thing although in central Africa our silver and china is rather scarce, and many of the other grandures of home. I did not go out to my district today.[16] I went to the English service in the evening, addressed by Dr. Laws.

April 3

... Mr. Stewart started at 9.0 am with the *Herga,* in tow of the *ilala,* for the east coast to explore up to the north end of the Lake ...

April 17 *First reference to recruiting men for start of road work – started north on May 2 from Bandawe*

May 26 *Reference to learning arithmetic on May 26 and algebra under Stewart's tuition.*

June 12 (Kasingula)

Wakened by the clamour of people around the camp. I rose and got ready for employing more people. I started one hundred and forty seven, there was a great many more wanting work, but had to be refused ...

---

[15] Although the 'Angoni', or more correctly 'Ngoni', were at one time regarded as an off-shoot of the Zulu of South Africa, they were simply two groups who spoke similar languages. They had a reputation for military organisation and ferocity.

[16] This indicates that all personnel associated with the mission were allocated an area for prosetelysation.

June 22
The natives are greatly astonished at seeing a lock, hinges, etc. on a door, they think I am a magician or something more wonderful, as I get everything to fit so well ... Ross's boy has run away today ... I have got a hen and duck house put up.

28 July (*Karambo*)
... Mr. Stewart and I went out with our guns for a short time. We killed 4 zebras and wounded some others ...[17]

July 30 (Sabbath)
At 4.0 am I was wakened by some animal at my tent door, I rose and fired at it, it went off with a groan. At daybreak we could see nothing but a few stains of blood. The day was spent reading Kingsley's sermons.

Aug 1
When going to my work I found a large leopard lying dead within thirty yards of my tent this being the animal that I fired at on Sabbath morning. I could not make use of the skin as it had already begun to decay ...

Aug 5
Wakened by a lion and a hyena keeping up a melody near my tent ...

Aug 12
... I killed a splendid eland the horns being 3 ft 6 inches long, and the skin rather a pretty one. I am going to preserve the skull and horns.

Aug 13
Last night the hyenas stole the skin of the eland ...

Aug 22
All the men struck work, owing to one of the men being turned away. They came running along the road yelling and shouting, like as many schoolboys after a game at shinty. After breakfast I had a long chase after buffalo, but without success. On my return, I was astonished to hear that Kangoli (that is a chief that has been routed out of his village by the Angoni, and is now resident here) was informed that we were going to make war with him. So he came up with all his men to see if it was true. I expect it was the doing of some slavers that is here on a visit and these are the reports that they generally carry with them from place to place. It is more profitable for them to have all the chiefs hostile to one another and make war if possible, and they will buy the prisoners. We have to be continually on our guard against these fellows.

---

[17]   Although Munro and others hunted for meat for themselves and their men, there are frequent references to shooting that went well beyond their requirements, and they seemed to have little concern for wounding animals in the process.

Sept 9
Got on remarkably well with the work, paid some of the men. In the afternoon, the chief here (Wyanga) had a great quarrel with my men. They got rather hot on the matter, they were about to attack one another with spears, when I interfered and stopped it, for if I would stand and look on it would get myself into trouble, as my fellows would be called my children (this being the native way of expressing it) or wage war to the bitter end.

Sept 12
Started other ten men. About 8.00 am a company of traders passed, going east. There were forty-five in all, heavily laden with calico and well armed[18] ... At 2.00 pm I sent six men to the lake for picks and crowbars. In the evening I killed a snake six feet long, it was at the side of my tent.

Sept 14
... At 2.00 pm I killed another large serpent at my tent. It was about a foot longer than the last. They are very numerous here. I bought a little dog for to keep me in amusement.

Oct 7
Got part of the men started to work, principally those that were not able to go to war, I paid 177 yards to workers. In the afternoon I went out to hunt a crocodile but could not get him out of the deep water. I am longing very much for the mails as they are overdue.

On Nov 6 *M starts from Karambo for Maliwanda/Chiringi.*

Nov 29
... At dinnertime, I tried for the first time to churn. My churn was a tea tin, being so far successful as to make a pound of butter, it being the first manufactured in this part of the country by a European ...

Dec 25 (*Chiringi*)
This being Christmas, we had no way to celebrate it but by a hard day's work, so I got started to the windows of the house. At 11.50 two men arrived with the remainder of our mails. And to my great astonishment there were no less than twelve letters and about twenty papers being in all with this mail seventeen home letters and seven local, and about twenty-two newspapers ... I was very sorry to hear of Mary's sickness and also of little Jennie Mackintosh's ...

Dec 31 Sabbath
The most of the day spent reading the Christian Herald. In this manner was the last day of the year spent. And when I look back and think what have I been doing for my Creator in this land of heathen darkness for the last twelve months, well may I blush and say that I have been looking more to my own selfish interest, and forgetting to strive to advance

---

[18]   Calico cloth was used universally as currency: apparently the Livingstonia Mission expended 15 miles of calico in one year. It could be plain or printed.

the cause of my great Master. But my prayer is that on entering another year, that I may enter anew to the work of the spread of the Gospel.

Jan 10 - 30 December 1883 'This has Caused a Shadow to Fall on Us All'

Jan 10

Got finished with paving of cattle house. In the afternoon Mr. Stewart wished us to try and get the bullocks nostrils pierced. I got a hold of the first and tumbled it, after fastening it. I was made doctor and the instrument I had to use was a small tin tube, and with a strong stroke of the hammer cut a fine round hole in the nostrils: we got three of then cut. (my first attempt to doctor cattle)

Jan 12

... In the evening we had a bit of fun, we got a hold of the old bullock (called Tom) for to get his nose pierced. We got him drawn in close to a tree, but he had a great suspicion of us, thinking that we were after some mischief. After he considered his position, he got angry at the idea of being martyred in that fashion, he sprang at the tree and almost broke it—at his second attempt broke the rope, and set him at liberty. We then managed to pierce the nose of another young bull. We then tried to get a yoke on a pair of them but it turned out a difficult task. After a long time of running and fighting with them we had to stop, until we could get an erection made, to fasten them in so as to yoke them. (*They eventually succeeded in piercing the noses of all the cattle and getting them yoked to draw a roller along the road.*)

Jan 15

All the men came up today to have a talk with the Asunga (white men) They wanted to be our children, and that we would fight their battles, etc. but this of course we could not agree to...

Feb 4

... at 3.0 am The herd came running and calling out that the wild beasts were killing the cattle. Messrs Stewart and Ross went at once to see what was wrong. It happened to be a leopard, it killed a sheep and pulled it a considerable distance, and then ran away. Ross took part of the flesh and put 4 grains of strychnine in it and laid it where the leopard left the sheep ...

March 5

... This morning, the boy announced the birth of a calf ... When at dinner the cry was raised, a leopard amongst the cattle, we out at once in pursuit of it, the cattle were within two hundred yards of the house, the herd said the young calf was gone. We went in the direction he was seen to go. Mr. Stewart's English terrier followed us out and apparently got the scent of the leopard, as he darted away in front of us. And in a few moments, within eighty yards of us, we heard him give a shrill squeal, we hurried to the place but could see nothing ... After searching all around were about turning home when Mr. Stewart saw the footprints of the leopard at the bed of the small stream. We traced him to a small thicket near at hand. Maryjan was approaching it said he saw the leopard in the thicket. We drew our revolvers and entered, there we saw the poor dog with the head half eaten. We fired a couple of shots into the densest of the thicket but no signs of any creature moving. We then had a walk around it, I was going to the upside again, when I saw the monstrous animal making his way out of the thicket. I gave the alarm and fired. He trotted gently off, we saw him again rising over a small hill. We fired a few shots but apparently to no effect – if we had our guns we might have had a fair chance of killing him – he was an exceptionally large one and pretty dark in colour.

March 17 *Having left Chiringi on 12 March, Munro meets up with steamer at Kasingula and hears that Monteith Fotheringham[19] has been badly spiked in a game trap, with a wound of 7 inches in his thigh, and has had to recuperate over 6 weeks. On the same day returning home, Munro was almost swept away in a flooded river being about half an hour in the water, his 'worst experience' to date.*

March 20

... The steamer sailed at 11 am. As I got a clothes and tool box up from Bandawe, I began to arrange my clothes in my boxes, but when I came to my tool chest, I was horrified to see the mounds of earth in it over my tools. On overhauling all my tools, I find that there is about twelve pounds worth destroyed by the white ants, all through McCallum's carelessness in whose charge I left the box ...

April 4

Had a dreadful night with wind and rain – I had to go out in the midst of it and secure my tent. Sent word to Karamba for men, he promised to give men in the course of a fortnight, I can give them work if they come as I have little faith in their promises. A messenger arrived with letters, stating that the steamer arrived last night, having Mr. Johnston of the University Mission on board, who is going to the north end of the lake.

April 5 *(Leaves Karambo for Maliwanda)*

I wanted two of the Livingstonia fellows to start for Maliwanda, this they refused. As I happened to ask a would be something of the name of Jonathan, who knows the way, so they lifted their gear and cleared out, one of their number and an Ajawa volunteered to go. Later in the day the runaways came back, asking to be forgiven, etc. It is something horrible to think of the deceitfulness of these fellows, who get the name in our records etc. of Christianised natives, I am sorry to think that their small bit of civilisation only helps them in their crafty deceitfulness.

---

[19] L. Monteith Fotheringham, a burly red-haired ex-shipyard foreman from the Clyde, was known by his men as 'Thunder and Lightning' for his roaring temper: He was much disliked by McEwan for his rough manners. His book *Adventures in Nyasaland* (1891) details his involvement in the 'Arab Wars'.

19 April *Munro refers to the difficulty of making the road through splintered rock without blasting materials, working only with crowbars.*

April 20

The native food still very scarce, it is with great difficulty that I can get a fowl. I feel very lonely this while back, and I have no desire for food. This cause may arise from the fact that most of my goods are old stores and in no way tasty. Considering everything, I have a great desire to leave the country, as I believe it would be to my benefit.[20]

May 9 (*Karambo*)

While at dinner the boy came in and said four men passing and they are in slave sticks.[21] I went to the tent door and there was the four poor fellows, with the sticks fastened round their necks, each carrying a load. Had I the power to release these poor wretches from their merciless dealers, how gladly would I execute that duty. The country seems to be overrun with slave hunters the last twelve months or more, and they seem only to be increasing. I cannot get a fowl to buy I had a man away this last two days and could get none.

May 23

... About 8.0 am I got a pleasant surprise, by being told that the mail arrived. On opening the bag I got five letters from Mother, one from America, one from Govan, two from Ardrishaig and eight papers and a few local letters. I was also informed that the steamer was returning tomorrow morning and I was not ready with my home mail, so I'll have to sit up all night writing.

May 26 *M refers to walking with Monteith and getting home news from him, including from Free St Mary's Govan of which they were both members and also a reference to the carriage of the first consignment of the LMS steamer to Tanganyika.*[22]

June 1

... I had a letter informing me that the storemen at the lake has been helping themselves to some cloth. It is the great misfortune of this country that trustworthy fellows cannot be got, to look after any European goods, and all this is by the so-called Christianised natives.

---

[20] This is the first time that Munro, an otherwise resolute pioneer, expresses homesickness, almost certainly from a combination of isolation, poor food, and frequent fever.

[21] Forked sticks round the neck, often joined similarly to another slave, making it virtually impossible to escape and dangerous to move on uneven ground.

[22] The London Missionary Society had been persuaded by Stevenson to use this route for the transport of their first steamer on Lake Tanganyika, a formidable undertaking, largely supervised by Monteith Fotheringham.

June 7

Spent a pleasant evening with Mr. Monteith, he slept in my tent. He was very anxious for an early start, I could scarcely persuade him to stay for breakfast, he left about 7 am. Two of his carriers ran and left him ...

June 21

Despatched two men to the lake for calico, another was sent to buy fowls. About 11 am he turned, sweating all over, without either fowls or cloth. He told me that the Arabs took the cloth from him and sent him away. I thought to let such things go on with impunity would be my ruin here, and the sooner it would be stopped the better. Taking with me two men, my guns and revolver, I started for this encampment. On reaching the houses or huts, we entered inside a sort of stockade, the fellow from which the cloth was taken being first. As soon as they saw him carrying a gun, the five fellows that was there flew up and sang out for their guns and spears. When they saw me their ardour cooled down a little. I asked where was the cloth, they denied ever seeing it. Still they were anxious for their guns. One of them went to shove past me to get his gun, I threw him back and drew my revolver and told them they would not get out of that till they gave up the cloth. I saw at once that the revolver was the proper to show them, as one of them sprung into the house and brought the cloth. They all fell down at my feet clapping their hands being the native way of paying homage. They also wanted to present me with three or four fowls, if I would spare their lives. I had little intention of taking their lives, but knowing them to be cowards I wanted to frighten them, and would take none of their fowls. We came away and left them in great consternation, hoping this will teach them that they cannot interfere with impunity with our goods or men ...

June 29 (*Maramura*)

All the men turned out to work, they grumbled greatly at having to cut so deep in the rock. I hope to get out soon with this deep cutting, the road has to be made in the face of a rock that has been eaten away with the stream.[23] The man that I sent to the lake for cloth returned without either cloth or letter.

30 June

... after stopping work at midday, I counted the picks and crowbars, three crowbars were missing. The men were ordered to search for them, as they would get no pay till they were found. They returned after two or three hours searching: they found them about two miles away hid in the grass. I paid them in white calico as no prints were sent up.

July 7 (*Viraura Hill*)

... we had work paying the men as we could not give them the cloth they wanted, it was four o'clock before we got them all away. Maramora came with a goat and a sheep to buy medicine (war medicine) of us. We gave him a large quantity of cloth as a present

---

[23] This section created great roadbuilding difficulties, with only primitive tools to construct deep earthworks on steeply-sloping rocky ground.

and also as payment for the sheep and the goat, but as we would not give medicine he threw down the cloth and took away his sheep and goat. His son afterwards took the cloth, but gave nothing in return.

July 13

... At dinner time Karamba and a few of his right hand men came with a calf and some fowls for us. He was promised a truss of calico if he could give plenty of men to make the road to Mwinicheranga's. He was very anxious to get war medicine. They won't believe us when we tell them we have no such medicine, only our guns. They believe that it is this medicine that they believe we have does all our wonderful deeds.

July 16

... At twelve noon two men arrived with a letter bearing the sad news of Capt. R. M. Gowans death. On Mr. Stewart's arrival they got him carried from the steamer to the house. About midnight they thought he was dying, but he again rallied a little, they thought he was falling off to sleep when day broke, but alas he never awoke and passed away in silence, without a word. They buried him outside the village under a baobab tree. This is another warning to us, to be ready against that day when our call will come. Mr. Stewart has kindly given me the loan of his watch till I may get my own.

July 18

... Mr. Monteith arrived here in the evening. Mr. Stewart advised him to come up for a change as he has not been very well for the last two weeks or so. I am real glad at the prospect of having his company for a few weeks, and hope that the change will do him good.

July 19

At a very difficult part of the road, we have to build up a wall twelve or fifteen feet high, and put the road on it, as we have no means of removing a very hard projecting rock that is in the way.

Aug 4

The workers seemed quite delighted with the quality and quantity of cloth they got. After getting clear of the workers I spent the afternoon assisting Mr. Monteith who has bought a great quantity of ivory from the Arabs, it is pretty difficult to deal with them.

Aug 16

After coming home in the evening I had a visit from Mlozi[24] the Arab who has camped at Karamba's village for the last number of months, being on his way upcountry. After speaking for a few minutes, he said 'I am going to say prayers but

---

[24] Mlozi was one of the most powerful and intransigent of the slavers, who in the later 'Arab Wars' resisted to the last and was eventually executed by the British (see also references in McEwan's diary).

Mlozi, Arab Slave Trader at Karonga Stockade, on Visit

Will be back again.' After supper he came along with a great number of his follow-ers, he has also brought his music box (the one I repaired) to enliven the conversa-tion. When they entered the tent they took off their sandals, and kept on their caps 'the real eastern fashion.' They sat and talked for about two hours or so. They wanted to know if I would live at peace with them, etc. I told them we were not here to make war with people, but if we are interfered with, then we will use our guns in our defence. They seemed to be very intelligent fellows, and know a great deal about the country.

Aug 21
After coming home from work about 6.0 pm the mail arrived having three home and four local letters for me ... I was sorry to hear of Mrs Duncan, Blantyre, who died 24 June 1883 from the effects of dysentery. And also a Mrs Nicol who had newly arrived with her husband (Blantyre school master) – she died in childbed 11 June 1883 after a day or two of illness.

Aug 22
... when coming home from work, I was met by five wild boars, the dog charged at them, I drew my revolver being the only weapon of defence I had. The men were all behind – when they saw me they made to run away, but the dog irritated them, so they all rushed at him and the dog ran back to me for protection, the largest of the boars followed him. I fired and the animal turned, the second time he pushed at me instead of the dog. I faced up and when the animal made to turn I lodged a bullet in his leg. He made another

attempt but only got another shot, so he made a final race at me with his mouth wide open. When within two yards of me I fired at his head and he fell like lead. By this time one of the men came up. I took his spear and tried to thrust it in the brute, but no the spear curled up. I got my pocket knife thrust in him. The rest parlayed a quick retreat when their champion fell, he is a fine large animal and the first I have killed ... The men were very proud of their booty as they are fond of such nyama (meat).

Aug 24 (*Maramora*)
... Mr. Stewart had a bad night's fever accompanied by jaundice, he was unable to leave his bed ... in the afternoon Moir, Pulley and Roxburgh arrived on their way to Tanganyika, the latter remaining there, the two former returning when they get settled about the carrying over of the steamer.

Aug 26
Mr. Stewart much worse and highly coloured (yellow). I spent a pleasant day with Mr. Roxburgh who has come from Govan, under the auspices of the London Missionary Society.

Aug 27
Started one hundred and five workers. Mr. Stewart no better ... I had to stop the workers and work for a day or two as Mr. Stewart required me to look after him, he is also very bilious, he can take a little food.

Aug 28
Mr. Stewart still very weak, I got a hammock rigged up outside so that he might get the fresh air about him. He spent most of the day outside. When I was taking him in about 3 pm, he fainted in my hands ...

Aug 30
Mr. Stewart appeared to be much the same in the morning, he took a biscuit and a little soup. But the hiccup which continued since Tuesday night was in no way abated, he became quite unconscious and talked about houses and bricklaying ... at 11.25 am I saw him in the easy chair I hurried to him, he began to groan very loud, and gasping for breath. I thought he was in a faint so I put a little water on his face and hands. But at last I saw it was the death struggle. We got him lifted into bed, where he breathed his last immediately afterwards. He died at 11.30 am on 30 August 1883, apparently in great agony. He did not utter a single word. Little did I think when I saw him last Thursday, that he would be a corpse the day ... I wanted some of the natives here to come, and carry the body to the lake so that we could get him buried beside Capt. Gowans. But they all ran away to the bush so that I have to wait for my own men. I got the body dressed and sown up in a white sheet, as I have neither wood or nails for a coffin. At 4.10 pm Mr. Stewart's boy Patris and other two men arrived from Maliwanda's ... I showed them the body covered in the tent. Poor Patris burst out the crying like a child, he is the first black fellow I ever saw shedding a tear through grief.

Aug 31(*Kasingula*)

... we started for the lake with the body. After committing all the clothing he was using during his illness to the flames ... I got the men to dig the grave which was six feet deep ... we buried him beside Capt. Gowans under the same baobab tree ... a great number of the natives assembled to witness the funeral.

Sept 27

At 2.00 pm the steamer was sighted ... an hour afterwards she cast anchor on the beach. She also had on board Rev. Professor H. Drummond of F.C.C. Glasgow,[25] also Rev. Mr. Bain who is to take charge of the mission station at Maliwanda's.[26] He has come merely to see the country and to take a report of the same to Dr. Laws who is going home soon. Mr. Drummond has come on a visit to this country to see what the country can produce. He is going to Tanganyika then returning home

Nov 12 *(Maramora)*

... Mr. Moir anxious that I should take charge of a caravan to Tanganyika, I agreed to assist him. He led me to understand that the road will go on, and that I'll have the working of it.

Nov 19

... Mr. Drummond made a great discovery, in the hill that I have been cutting the road in, he got a fossil of a fish and a variety of scales of fish.

23 Nov *M says he could hardly sleep after reading of 'the sad account of the fearful disaster in Messrs Stephens and Son Yard, Linthouse, Govan as I was personally acquainted with a number of the sufferers.'*

Dec 3 *(M hunting elephants at north end of lake)*

At 1.30 we sighted the animal. Pulley and I went to the left, Moir and Berry to the right. We opened fire putting four shots into his left side, the other put two in his right, the animal turned round and Pulley gave him another shot in the head and he fell dead ... he had a fine pair of tusks weighing 43 pounds. When on the way home, I killed a buffalo calf, a great demand on the meat.

Dec 8

... the lake was alive with hippos. We killed two and wounded three or four ...

Dec 13

After coffee in the morning, Messrs. Moir, Pulley and Berry and I went down to the stream to wash ... the water was rather muddy so we only went in about 4 yds from the

---

[25] Professor Henry Drummond had been commissioned by James Stevenson to carry out a scientific survey of the area around the proposed route of the road and wrote up his experiences in *Tropical Africa* which sold 20,000 copies by its 3rd edition.

[26] This station seems to have been located here primarily because of its proximity to the Stevenson Road, but was not otherwise regarded as convenient.

bank, in about 2ft of water. We were enjoying ourselves swimming, etc. when Berry who was within 2 yds of me screamed, the next moment he was pulled under water by a monstrous crocodile. We could do nothing for him as he was pulled out to midstream, Pulley ran for a gun, but ere it came, he was pulled under the water for the last time, as he did not reappear again we followed the bank down for a mile or more but could find no trace of him. The crocodile caught him first by the leg and pulled him into the deeper water, then he caught him by the left arm, having shoulder and breast in his monstrous jaws, Berry appeared to be then unconscious, as his head lay resting on the upper jaw. He had only come to this country a few months ago for a while's shooting, he was captain of the Natal Frontier Light Horse. We set the natives to work to try and get the body, during the search, 5 crocodiles were killed, one of them measured 13ft by twenty eight inches broad, length of jaws 23 inches. I have great reason to thank God that it was not me that was taken, as I was further out a minute or so before that. This has caused a shadow to fall on us all. (*in a note at the top of the diary page M has added 'I tried to get his hand, but he swung his tail – I sprung out of the water and let myself fall forward and also toward the bank.'*)

Dec 14
We sold by auction part of Capt. F. H. Berry's goods. In the afternoon Pulley and I went out after game. We were fortunate enough to bag two buffaloes, one reed buck, two black eiders, two quails, one snipe ...

15 Dec *M describes knocking over seven elephants in two minutes, when the boys were sent across the river to kill some more.*
'Pulley got sharply along the bank and got the elephants crossing and made a fine slaughter of the large elephants ...'

Dec 16
Took a walk out to see the elephants, we counted 19, one being without tusks. We than had a nice bathe in the lake.[27]

Dec 17
Sent the boys out to bring in the ivory, they returned bringing in 42 tusks, weighing 342 lbs. That being 22 elephants in all that we killed in less than an hour and a half, being the largest number on record in this part of the country. Pulley shot a fine large hippo in the evening.
(*the next few pages are filled with descriptions of game hunts and large scale killing*)

---

[27] It seems astonishing that after the manner of Berry's death, they should even consider this.

Ivory caravan of the African Lakes Company

Dec 30

... After four hours very hard walking, we reached the camp, and glad we were to find Crawshay in life, although very weak. After our arrival he pulled round a little, his complaint being dysentery. I think he will get over it yet, he has lost all hope himself of getting better. He told us what was to be done with his effects, etc. Mr. Moir's dog was bitten by a serpent, and was in spasms for about half an hour. After rubbing him and working with him, he came round and appeared all right. As I was sitting up with Crawshay, I heard a noise about 11 pm and was told that the dog was again in his fits, so I sat still, till I heard Moir calling out that he was caught by the dog. I ran to his assistance at once, seized the dog by the throat until he let go Mr. Moir's arm – I was told to hold on in case he would rush at any of us. By the time I released my hold, the dog was dead. Mr. Moir burned the wounds. Boys shot a male leopard the other day.[28]

---

[28] This is typical of the laconic way Munro describes a hectic day of incident

6 February - 31 December 1884: A New Engineer

Feb 6 *(Maramora)*
... I am a poor unfortunate, I have no less than twelve sores poulticed between hands and feet, some of them have formed into nasty ulcers ...

Feb 7 *(Chiringi)*
This is my twenty sixth birthday, how slowly yet how swiftly the time goes on. I have seen many changes since my last birthday, some of those with whom I have associated has been called away I hope to the better land, others had to leave the country through ill health, how thankful I should be that God is so merciful to me ...

Feb 26
Taking an inventory of the road goods, find that a good deal has been stolen since September last, must have been taken by the late storemen. As I was turning out the needles, there were no less than twenty packages short ...

Feb 28
Got finished with the arrangements of goods, etc. Bought a few cat skins. Killed a large fish eagle. Made a nice rolly-polly.[29]

March 14 *(Karonga)*
I am greatly pained with small water blisters all over the groin, I am at a loss to know what it can be, I have no doctor to consult ... killed a pair of large snakes.

March 17
... Killed a monstrous large snake 7ft 1 inch long, girth six inches – it was in a tree direct above the path, leading from the house to the lake, it had almost touched heads of people as they passed. The natives say he is a most venomous one. Made my first attempt at sketching with colour.

April 6
Had a dreadful night with toothache. (sic!) I tried various things to stop it, Morphia and Morphia and Arnica and a few other things, but of no use, the pain deadened a little by breakfast time. I felt quite miserable all day.

April 12
... the conversation (*with the local chief Maramora*) caused me to enquire into the forms of marriage. Each man who wants to get married has to have some cloth, a hoe, and a cow wherewith to buy his wife. The value of a woman is a cow, nothing less can buy one. In this way the chiefs can buy dozens of them. While the majority of the young men can not get married for want of cows, and any young man who breaks this law is

---

[29] This amusing conjunction of disparate events is typical of a pioneer's daily life.

generally killed by the father-in-law, and those who are left widows are to remain widows, this is apparently the law but I am of the opinion that it is seldom put in force.

April 19
Went along to the Rukuru to have another go at the alligators, killed two, one was very long measuring fifteen feet, the other only about nine. It was fine to see the large one rolling in the water like a propeller after he got the second shot, I cut his skull right through with the bullets. The natives eat their flesh, particularly the young ones. I sold my shotgun to Salhum for sixty pounds of ivory, he has been trying to purchase it for the last month, but would not come up with the price. I bought a great quantity of porkupines' quills ...

April 26
... I was astonished to hear Patris's widow calling for one of my boys. I was rather curious to know what was the matter, as her child was crying bitterly. After watching for a while, I saw another man and Ralata take the child and go in the direction of the grave. (Patris's grave) Shortly after, others followed, bearing something in their hands. I waited their return and asked what they were doing. They said Patris's spirit was tormenting the child, and it would not rest, but crying every day, so they went to the grave to give food to his spirit, so that it might rest at peace. They took a dish of beer and a dish of flour and buried it at the grave, and of course the child was taken to see that the spirit of the father was not neglected. The child is cutting teeth, and this I believe they know, but a number of the men gets the foolish creature to make the beer that they may drink it, there is but a small quantity of it goes to the grave. The people are great beer drinkers. The petty chief that is over this village, I seldom see him sober.

May 7
Men arrived from Chiringi, with word that Mr. Moir is going to start overland from Bandawe Tuesday first, he wanted up Mr. Stewart's instruments for taking observations on the way down ... I am sorry that I am not accompanying him as I am perfectly tired here (*Karonga*) doing nothing.

May 9
The rainy season seems to be now over as we have had very little rain for the last fortnight. Out after butterflies about midday, they are rather scarce, the rest of the day at Arithmetic.

May 10
Felt quite miserable owing to the steamer not turning up. I am learning from sad experience that the hardest work is to have no work to do.

May 12
At 12.30 the steamer sighted. On coming nearer I saw that the flag was at half mast ... Mr. Harkness came ashore and gave me the following sad news from the south. Mr. Oftedahl who was acting captain of the steamer died at Bandawe 29 January 1884 from

dysentery. Also Mr. Fenwick who was elephant hunting on his own behalf, went down to Quilimane with a cargo of ivory. He took a tusk or tusks for a chief (Chipatula) on the lower river. On his return, he paid Chipatula in cloth and Chipatula was not satisfied with the amount of cloth he received and some high words passed between them. Chipatula fired at Fenwick and missed, Fenwick drew his revolver and shot his opponent dead. He discharged the other chambers of his revolver amongst Chipatula's retainers, after which he was caught and killed by Chipatula's son, and his head stuck up on the stockade. All Fenwick's men were also killed. This happened on the 13th or 14th February.[30] Thereafter war broke out in all directions. The Chief at Matopi threatened Harkness, so he was in great danger of his life, as his boys deserted him, and were plotted to take his life. He steamed away from Matopi just in time to save himself from Chagaru the Chief who arrived with a company of armed men, and as he was too late for the steamer he set fire to one of the store houses, and broke and destroyed all the goods lying there, the most of which belonged to the London Missionary Society ...

On 20 May *Munro left on the steamer from Karonga for Bandawe*
(Harkness then describes how Gowk on the Lady Nyassa was decoyed, the vessel was sunk in deep water, Gowk escaping only with what he wore: the company and all others are short of calico and provisions. Also word of another Civil Engineer in Mr. Stewart's place, now on his way here.)[31]

June 19 *(Mandala)*
Busy slinging parts of the boiler of the LMS steamer on wheels so that it can be taken to Matopi.[32]

June 21
Got all the boiler on the carts. In the afternoon Gowk and I were acting hairdressers. In the evening were invited to tea by Mrs Scott. All the Blantyre Mission people were present, spent a pleasant evening together. Mr. Scott spoke at length on how best to win the natives and have them in subjection. He believed in the reign of love, I differed from him on the subject.[33]

June 25
Had a splendid sermon from Mr. Scott on Luke xxii and 23rd. Had a nice address from him in the evening.

---

[30] There are various versions of this incident. Fenwick was at this time employed by the Church of Scotland Mission at Blantyre. It was not unusual for staff to become involved in trading on their own account.

[31] This of course was William McEwan.

[32] This is a very laconic description of what must have been a very difficult operation, to say nothing of its transport to Lake Tanganyika.

[33] An interesting reflection on Munro's more hard-headed attitudes towards dealing with local people, born of his own experience.

June 26 *(Matopi)*

... We got back to the river about seven o'clock. The hippos were in large numbers where we had to cross. I fired several shots among them, it did scatter them a little but not sufficient to insure safety in crossing. At last we ventured in the canoe, and made for across as quietly and quickly as possible, I took the precaution to loose my shoes and tie my rifle that if we were upset I might gain the bank. I was real glad when we got across.

July 11 (Blantyre) *Munro meets Mr. Morrison who told him of the difficulties they had had with natives on the way down to Morambala, when they refused firewood and threatened to capture the steamer. (This is also described in McEwan's diary.)*

Mr. McEwan has come up with them, he will be in the evening. After coming back I was introduced to Mr. McEwan, I think a great deal of him as he is a free and homely in his ways.[34]

After an alarm about lions waiting to attack cattle at Mandala station, Munro, Moir, and McEwan went after them unsuccessfully.

July 18 *(Mandala)*

Finished the flooring of the nursery. Mr. Moir told me that Capt. Foot would take in hand the punishing of Robert. *(a storeman accused of stealing)*

July 19

... At 11.0 am the herd came in saying that a lion killed a goat. We took our guns and went out as it was quite near to Mandala House. After quarter of an hour sharp walking we saw an animal running away through the grass. The boys said it was a lion. After a whiles search we got no less than five goats that were killed – there must have been more than one to have made such a slaughter in such a short time ...

Aug 4 *(Matopi)*

... at 12 noon Mr. McEwan arrived pretty much worn out, as he was not clear of fever he had to keep bed for the rest of the day.

Aug 18 *(en route to Karonga overland from Mandala)*

... Then I came to Makambira's village ... he complained of being harassed by the Angoni ... I am sure that a thousand men, women, and children turned out to have a look at the *Msungu* (white man) as I am the first or else the second white man that has been in his village ... my tent was soon surrounded by a noisy crowd who was most anxious to watch everything I did and said. I gathered up my sleeves to wash – a murmur of astonishment went through the crowd, at seeing such a white skin, my face being very brown with the sun. I then gave them a look at their own faces, and especially the women

---

[34] This editor's interpretation of 'free' here is belonging to the Free Church of Scotland, like Munro. Given the social and professional distinctions of the time, Munro may have been pleasantly surprised that McEwan - who is always referred to as *Mr* McEwan - was also 'homely.'

with large lip rings, they seemed to be ashamed of them when they saw them in their own lips as they tried to cover them with their fingers.

Aug 25 *(Deep Bay)*
... after climbing a bit I got a splendid view of Mount Waller, I never saw a finer looking mountain, it rises in spectacular terraces from the lake to the summit, the top being a level ridge, then cuts off in another terrace or two, it must have been heavy landslips or earthquakes that has given the mountain its present form ... after looking for a while I saw a huge animal looking down from a hill top, with his large ears going as if in search of a sound. I was a little puzzled to know what sort of a brute it was, as I could only see him dimly through the grass. He moved his head, then I saw the horns on his nose and knew that it was a rhino, till the track took me into long grass. I had not courage to follow further, as it is said that he is the only animal that will attack a person without provocation ...

Aug 28
Sent to Mapulira asking when the men would be back with the prisoners. He returned the answer this, you have given me no cloth in a present, and the thieves are off to the hills. I was so provoked that I walked off without a guide and soon lost the proper path, after regaining and walking on thinking how could I catch the thieves, when down I went into a game trap, I knew at once where I was and spreading out my hand broke the fall. I took a quick and anxious to see if there were any stakes under me. Seeing there were none I made a brave struggle and got out much better than a buffalo could do, the pit was something like eight feet deep. The men all ran back when they saw me dive in. Just as I got out, one of my men came up with a guide. These traps are very dangerous when put this way on the caravan roads.[35]

Aug 30 *(arrived at Karonga)*
... near midday we reached the pretty village of Kiyuni which is now a ruined heap of ashes, this being the handy work of the Angoni, who a month ago made a raid, killing fifteen women and one man, the cowardly lot. They however left four of their number to swell the number of the slain. We found the people huddled together amongst the reeds at the lake side, a pitiful sight, the reeds being tied together to form a roof over them, they seemed wonderfully happy notwithstanding their difficulties ... found Mr. McEwan (who had just arrived from Maliwandas) in good health. Mr. Nicol down with fever ...

Sept 1
... Mr. McEwan down with fever.

---

[35] Munro was very lucky to survive this: the outcome might have been different if the trap contained a live animal.

Sept 5 *(Maramora)*

... started other 50 men on the work, making the road along the west of the Kamasa valley. Came to a very nasty cutting at a bend of the river, sent to the lake for more crowbars. Got on well with the work. Bagged another guinea fowl.

Sept 6

Other 20 or 30 men started work, got on very well with the heavy cutting although it is very dangerous owing to the rock being quite loose, and almost perpendicular. At 4 pm Mr. McEwan started for the hill to the south of Maramora for to take some observations ...

Sept 13

I have finished the reading of my Bible, read it through chapter by chapter, omitting the two books of the Chronicles hoping that I have profited by the course I have taken.[36]

Sept 16

Last night shortly after going to bed a hyena began to pipe loud and clear near our camp, we were all glad to hear him as we had a trap gun for him. As I could not sleep with the toothache, I was listening to every sound, several times I thought the hyena was about my tent. I fell into a light sleep, when I was awakened by an awful yell from one of my boys. The camp was soon astir, the cause of the alarm was that the hyena got a hold of the boy by the ear, he being covered with his cloth did not see the gentleman that took him by the ear. Next moment the brute was off with his cloth (and was never got) it only left his teeth marks in his ears ...

Sept 18 *(Kamasa Stream)*

... I am longing to see Mr. McEwan down ...

Sept 24

At 10 am Mr. McEwan arrived at the work. He looked rather seedy. He has not been at all well since he left here. I did not get on so well with the work, a great number of trees in the way and the axes are very blunt.

Sept 26

Mr. McEwan relining the road making it much steeper, the descent to the Kamasa being about 1 in 6, it does not look well. I had to return on the portion made today and take it to 10 ft broad, the rest of the road being at an average of 6ft wide he also proposes altering a part of the road I made, as the turns are too quick. I was keeping to orders not to go over 1 in 20 of a rise or fall, and to descend as little as possible, keeping to these orders I

---

[36] It is not clear whether a formal course of Biblical instruction is being referred to here or simply Munro's decision to read his Bible throughout.

had to go around every gully, causing the road in some places to be very crooked. (Theory is very good, but in many cases practice beats it.)[37]

Sept 30

... my big box arrived safe from the lake. After opening it, I was real glad at seeing my album I sat for a while looking at old and well-known faces, trying to think what change time might work before I could see them again. Taking time[38] for Mr. McEwan, he taking observations.

Oct 1

... I have no inclination for food since the native potatoes and fowls have run down. I do not care for rice and tinned meat. Feeling quite homesick. I think that our bad bread, bad flour and badly made, has helped this ... our men are complaining at us going so far from villages, as it will take them two days to go for food, it is a loss to us as well as trouble to them.

Oct 2

I am longing to hear from home, it being now three months since I had my last letter.

Oct 3

Had very hard work removing very heavy stones, and also building up one side of the road. At 6 pm the mail arrived, but we were thoroughly disappointed, there being no home letters, owing to the unsettled state of the country on the lower river, there has be no word from the lower river since I left Mandala ...we also had word of Capt. Foot's (British Consul at Blantyre) death. He died 16th September of liver complaint ... he leaves a widow and four or five of a family. Poor man, he used to boast that brandy did him no harm, but I am afraid that it may have been the cause of his death.

Oct 10 *(Maramora)*

... Mr. McEwan very bad with toothache, and also one of the workers ... I have a nasty pain in the stomach.

Oct 15

The men were knocked off work for a while by red ants, they lined the road for about a hundred yards and they were in great clusters, guarding every small hole along that distance while the rest marched in procession between the clusters. As soon as the men broke their ranks, they scattered over the whole road and made it everything but pleasant for the men. Those kind of ants are most vicious when they get a hold, they keep it, as I have often seen the head parting with the body before they would let go, The natives say they can kill an elephant, if so the process must be very slow ...

---

[37] This gives a picture of a road which is little more than a cleared track through difficult country, but also a mild sideswipe at McEwan's book learning as opposed to Munro's practical experience.

[38] Refers to measurement by time.

Oct 20

Working at a deep cutting on a very quick bend of the road. In the afternoon I returned with eight men to try and get out a large stone that projected out of the line of road. We had two men clearing the earth from it for the last week. After breaking a few heavy wooden levers trying to remove it, we had to let it remain in, as it take two days to have it removed. Monteith arrived making about 30 miles, he was rather tired, he marched all day on a cup of coffee, he being short of provisions. After supper we got the account of his journey to and from Tanganyika ... he seemed to be in a very discontented state of mind, finding fault with everybody and everything. nothing seemed to go right but what he did himself. He certainly has a great deal to complain of as to how he is treated by the managers of the company.

Oct 31 *(Lufira)*

... there is a war raging between the Portuguese and the Machingiri (late Matakenya) people.

Munro then quotes at length from a letter from F.T. Morrison which describes in some detail how the missionaries and ALC personnel got caught up in this uprising, with the intent of killing all whites, focussed on the district around Marua and Mopea. Although this became a serious affair, involving several thousand rebels, all the Europeans escaped with their lives, albeit some were wounded.

Nov 4

... At 1 pm the Rev. Mr. Harris of the London Missionary Society arrived at the work en route for Tanganyika. Mr. McEwan accompanied him to camp. In the evening he gave us all the down country news. He had the misfortune of being at Maruru at the time of the Machingiri war. He along with Mrs Hore and baby and other two missionaries from the same society were on their way to Tanganyika via Nyassa, the rest on hearing of the war left the country and returned to Natal and is now on their way to Tanganyika by Zanzibar and Ujiji.[39] They were joined by Capt. Hore. I am sorry that his coming this way will add nothing to its popularity as he said himself he was thoroughly disgusted with everything he heard and saw regarding the A.L. Coy. (the hearing being much more than the seeing) I am sorry that missionaries does not always carry a missionary spirit. I got tired of his fault finding tales.

Nov 14

The men made an early start and worked very hard, finishing over 500 yards by 11.30 am We joined the road with the native path alongside the River Lufira on the right bank, thus finishing this season 16 miles and all hill work or mostly ... The new road has now done away with the worst part of the native path between the two lakes. We are well satisfied with the amount of work done this season, as we managed far above our

---

[39]   This was the well established trade route from the coast to the interior used by the Society prior to the agreement with Stevenson.

expectation. On the whole it was very difficult work, and particularly the engineering part.

Nov 21 *(Karonga)*
Had a dreadful night with toothache, the pain was more than I can describe, I never thought that a person could suffer so much from toothache. I tried all sorts of available medicines, at last I tried a little brandy and quinine, it sickened me and after vomiting, the pain was not so bad ...

Dec 12
... At night we had a hot chase after rats in the store, killed 142. The Ajaw boys eat them, they take and singe them and set them over the fire to dry and smoke them.

Dec 15 *(Karambo en route to Tanganyika)*
After arriving here we sent for Karambo as we wished to give him a present of some cloth. After talking with him a little we asked for the men to take loads to Maliwanda's, he asked for cloth and would promise no men. So we at length gave him about 30 yds prints he then promised to get two men for us, and took the cloth as if he had a right to it or rather that he was doing us a favour by taking it, Africans have no gratitude in them.

Dec 16
At the Kamasa (in the hills) at 5.30pm our neat marching distance for the day being 3 hours 53 minutes distance being 12 miles 1132 yards – Total distance from lake 22 miles 958 yards. This distance is according to Mr McEwan's system of measuring. He measures the length of his pace and how many paces he takes per minute. This must give a very good idea of the neat distance travelled. I often check his paces by measuring them. My part of the work is to look after the carriers and do the shooting part of it, as it is very necessary to keep the men in food.[40]

On same day he records 17 miles 1083 yards being covered in 5 hours 55 minutes.

Dec 23
... At 12.15 we camped at Mwini Fuvia. I was very feverish and got my bed into an old hut till the tent would be pitched. Mr. McEwan heaped me with clothes so as to make me sweat, my pulse ranged from 140 to 150 beats per minute. After two hours in bed I began to sweat, so the men carried me to the tent ...[41]

---

[40]   Munro appears to have been responsible for obtaining food and managing the men, while McEwan was in charge of laying out the route and deciding on engineering aspects.
[41]   This is the first of several references to McEwan nursing Munro and their belief in the efficacy of sweating out the fever.

Dec 24

Unable to leave bed, had a bad night's sleep, and fearful dreams. My fever turned into jaundice, could take no food. If not better tomorrow, we are going to return to Chiringi (*Munro had to be carried back to Chiringi in a machila*) [42]

Machila transport

Over Christmas, both men were fevered. – by the 27th with Munro quite ill, the journey to Tanganyika was stopped, so that Munro could pass the rainy season at Bandawe and get some medical treatment there. He was also suffering from toothache. He has a very difficult journey back down to the lake and Karonga.

Dec 31

... I spent the last evening of the year chatting over bygone days and deeds, bringing old associates to our remembrance and making our hearts yearn to get once more back among them, but we cannot realise our wish in the meantime, we hope that after a few more months we may be preparing to leave this country. It is long to look to, but come it will, and I hope we may be spared to see it.

---

[42] *Machila* was a stretcher-like carrier, sometimes with a cover, supported usually by 4 porters. Note that despite his condition, Munro is still making diary entries at the time.

5 Jan - 8 May 1885: 'We are on our last loaf ...'

Jan 5

... At 6.0 pm we cast anchor at Bandawe harbour ... we learnt that Frederick had four fits since the steamer left for the north end, we found him very weak, so much so that he had to be told who I was before he could recognise me, he has been taking no food, and suffering from violent headaches. Mr. Smith who is at present up at Angoni land, has also been at death's door for the last week with fever, but is now fast recovering. Mrs Scott has been down for the last week with fever. I am sorry to learn that there is a general scarcity of food here as well as at the North end, everybody seems to be on their last tins of flour, sugar, etc. This dearth of European food is at present felt all over the country at Mandala as well as elsewhere, it is rather a serious state of matters, but I hope that they may soon take a turn for the better.

Jan 7

After breakfast I went over to the Doctor's to have a tooth extracted, as I have been troubled with toothache for the last three months. The Dr was rather frightened to try it in case it might go like the last one. He tried to prevent this, he sent the forceps down to the root of the tooth causing great pain, after a good wrench he got it out all right, it being a three-pronged one.[43] Had a while reading the life of the Prince Consort.

Jan 8

Sketching part of Bandawe station, afterwards trying to colour it. I find it rather a pleasant study, though rather difficult.[44]

Bandawe Station, Sketch by Donald Munro

---

[43] This operation was almost certainly conducted without anaesthetic.
[44] These sketches have survived in good condition, but are difficult to reproduce.

Jan 13

This is the day generally celebrated at home for the New Year (old New Year)—how I long to get back there again to join in their festivities. Got myself weighed 9 stone 8 pounds, that being a stone less than when here in August last year, and I am now doubtless much heavier than I was a week ago …

Jan 15

Shortly after going to bed last night I heard a noise something like the crying of a child. I heard it three times, but paid no attention to it. This morning the herd told me that two of the young goats were killed by leopard during the night, their bleating being the noise I heard, the Dr intend setting poison for it tonight, as the head of one of the goats were found. Painting up old sketches.

Jan 16

I spent a very pleasant evening with Dr. and Mrs Scott. I could not help envying the Dr's lot, as I have now often seen, that where a lady is there is the appearance of comfort and cleanliness, which makes a person feel that they are again in civilisation, not to make mention of the fine cakes and splendidly made food. This last is greatly needed to add to our comfort in this country.[45]

Jan 20 *After a bad bout of fever Munro comments on his appearance.*

… I am looking miserably bad, my eyes are sunk, my cheeks hollow, etc. etc. I hope that I may soon pull up to my usual state of health.

Jan 21

After going to bed last night … at 11.45 pm a noise like that of thunder pass the station. It lasted only for a second or two. I could not understand what the sound was, when the whole house shook, and the dishes rattled together, my bed shook very much, making a strange sensation creep over me. McCallum called out if I felt the earthquake. Upon asking about it this morning everybody agrees that it was the heaviest earthquake that they have yet felt at the station … in the evening I conducted the prayer meeting in the Dr's absence.

Jan 22

… I had a letter from Mrs Vartan (?) letting me know that she sent me the scarf, ring and that it was made by the people of Palestine. She also mentions that they are sending out an iron memorial tablet to place over the grave, it possibly may come with Dr. Laws when he returns to this country. She wishes a sketch of tree and grave … *Mrs Vartan was Stewart's sister then living in Palestine—the scarf ring almost certainly for his services to Stewart.*

---

[45]   There was a general belief that European food was necessary to maintain health: certainly it contributed to morale.

Jan 26

Trying to work out a sketch of the baobab at Mr. Stewart's grave to send to his sister, as she would like to get it. Repairing my little clock, failed in the attempt. In the evening I sketched out a plan for Dr. Elmslie's house in the hills.

Jan 30

... Messrs Smith and Sutherland arrived from the hills. They were both pretty much done up with the march, as they were cripples. Mr. Smith had to hire *mashila* men to carry him in today. All well on the hills, but Mission work meeting with no success. It seems to be the opinion of all that the Europeans are only allowed to remain on the hills among the Angoni for the sake of the presents that are regularly given by members of the mission. The head chief Mombera seems to have all the members of the mission under his thumb, particularly Koyi who he uses as his tool in begging from the other members. Certainly the past history of the Angoni mission has been a blank, and the future looks as black as the present.[46]

Feb 3 *(Banna)*

... I sent the medicine man and other two away to the forest in search of buffaloes, while I turned home. I saw some pigs and killed one. We reached a lagoon where there were some hippos enjoying themselves, I started firing at them. After a while's hot work, I had the satisfaction of knowing that at least one was dead, and am sure that more will share the same fate. In fever most of the day.

Feb 6 *(Bandawe)*

... In the evening there was a sale by auction in the Dr's house of the contents of a box sent by the foundry boys' society. The sale was conducted in rather a strange fashion. The best of the goods were put up and as they could not realise more than they could bring by private bargain, they were laid aside while the trashy stuff was bought at great profits to the Mission. The trashy stuff was sold first, or certainly they would not be bought afterwards.[47]

Feb 7

... This is my twenty seventh birthday, it has passed almost unheeded. Still it acts as milestones remembering me that I am quickly marching on through the journey of life, and my humble prayer is, that I grow in years I may also grow in grace and in the knowledge of my Lord and Saviour.

---

[46] McEwan appears to have concurred with this view and recommended either military suppression of this tribe or withdrawal.

[47] Donations of this kind from industrial workers, encouraged by the church, appear to have been quite common.

Feb 10

... I had the usual good news from home of all well, and of my brother Arch'd going to sea as carpenter on board the last boat that was built in the yard where he was employed in Kinghorn. He sailed November 14th on board the *Newcastle* for Sydney.

Feb 11

The first British Consulate flag was hoisted at the station today ... there is nothing but dissatisfaction on every face, as it has unfortunately turned out that neither flour nor sugar has been sent to any except Williams on the hills. Dr. Scott has been asked to petition Mr. Moir to send the steamer up another run without docking her, as we cannot live for three months on native *ufa* ...

March 5

... The longer I am in the country, the more I am convinced that the native is not to be trusted in anything. Tonight as the workers came home from the forest with the loose rope that they were out for, I counted them as they were passing and found that there were three absentees, so I called the roll, and this got the names of the truants, and the 'sort of foreman' went to plead ignorance in the matter, so and the others are to be fined. It is not customary to call the roll at nights, so they were caught in their deception.

March 7

... The steamer has not arrived as we expected, Mr. Morrison said if he would not be back today, he would not be until the steamer would be out of dock. If this is the case (as I hope not) it will be a sad affair with us here, we are on our last loaf, and the thought of being without bread for three months is everything but pleasant. (*The steamer did in fact arrive with provisions on 11 March.*)

March 9

... In the afternoon a woman came running to our cottage, crying most pitiful. I at first thought that she must have been bit by the donkey, but on coming up to see what was wrong, I learned that she was a slave that was released by one of the Mission boys about 6 months ago. She has since been staying out with Dan (one of the school teachers) – today her old master came to claim her and offered Dan a goat to give her up. Dan refused and the woman fled for the station. She apparently was sold to this man 6 months ago in exchange for another wife, and he wanted to take her to the island Chisamula where he belongs to. McCallum means to look after her safety and sent her back to Dan's. She is rather a nice looking woman with a child about a year old. The slaver I understand is to start some of these days across the lake with a fair number of slaves – it is a pity that a stop could not be put to this accursed traffic in this part of the country.

March 13

Gave another trial to the *Herga*, there was a heavy sea running, we could not steady the boat so as to get the stobs driven in. I lost my temper at one of the men who carelessly let the boat come across several times on the top of an old stob almost upsetting her, and then turning round and laughing at me. I gave him a crack or two with my hand, very much the same as I would do with a schoolboy. I was sorry afterwards, as I do not like the idea of lifting my hands to the natives. His companions seemed to say that he did not get the half of what he deserved, so they gave him the rest with their tongues.

March 19

After dinner I went over to the school, as I entered the door McCallum and Smith said there are two cases of smallpox in the school. I felt a little stunned at the news. On making further enquiry, it turned out to be what the natives call *mwana wa ntomba* (child of smallpox) ... The natives say that it is infectious and contagious, and that at present it is prevalent at Matiti and a number of people dying from it. There are also some cases near at hand. The only thing we can make out it is, is a kind of typhus fever. We strongly advised Smith to dismiss the boys that were suffering from it, and fumigate the school.

April 1

More cases of *kausi* – the most of the boarders asked to get home. Smith has taken back those who have had the fever rather soon, I am afraid he is not taking the steps he should to prevent the spread of the disease. He is retaining one or two of the boys that are in fever in the school, and the boys go and sleep in his cookhouse, so that they may be warmer. The Mission is greatly at fault in not having a hospital for sick boys ...

April 2

(*Dr. Scott*) thinks that the *kausi* is a kind of scarletina and will probably go over all the scholars ...

April 6 *(journey to Angoniland)*

... On passing Chikoko's village, my attention was drawn to what the chief unamwali (a young girl about 12 years or so) dance. I went to the ring – there the old women were dancing and singing to the best of their ability, led by the Chief's wife. The young girl was standing with a woman holding her blindfolded, like a statue. In another circle were the young men and women dancing, and I am sorry to say that all morality was laid aside by them and their dances are not a thing to be described on paper. These dances are what might be called marriage or a formal giving away of the bride and preparing her for all her future duty, etc ...

April 13 *Description of meeting the Ngoni Chief Mombera, also described by McEwan. Munro comments:*

I think the mission humbles itself too much to the usurpers (i.e. Angoni) and courts his friendship, which he is cunning enough to see, and consequently treats them in such a fashion, as is altogether contemptuous in my estimation. I cannot see how the heads of the mission could submit to sit for hours on end on an anthill in a dirty cattle kraal under a broiling sun. I never visited a chief of any consequence, but what he offered a seat in the shade, and gave a present for present, etc. I have often asked myself the question why should a handful of men who are the terror of all around them and who are never at ease except when they are robbing and plundering small outlying villages like these be regarded with such esteem, when other peaceable people are overlook. Highway robbery and murder is put down with a strong hand at home, why not do all in our power to do the same here.[48] *Munro was amused by the Chief's wife asking how Queen Victoria was* ...

April 20 *(Kambombo) Munro makes first ref to tsetse fly which are abundant and were likened to a Scottish cleg.*

April 21
... At Chikuta's village on the bank of the Wira stream ... the chief sent up a present of some *ufa* and a splendid sheep. We sent a return present of 8 yards of calico. My new table boy was caught stealing some maize cobs from the tent, so I gave him a thrashing that he won't forget in a hurry, and I am afraid the cook told him to do it. We got the sheep killed.

April 25 *(journey from Kambombo to Maliwanda)*
... Tonight has crowned all our wants, having been for the last few days out of sugar, tea, flour, and jam, we are now out of salt and tomorrow will finish our coffee. The sooner we get to our destination the better, as this is a serious state of affairs.

April 27
Very cold – thermometer down to 50.4. Some of the villagers came up and started their last night's pranks, of telling us a lie, then laughing at us. I gave the ringleader a drive with the toe of my boot, which had the desired effect ...

April 28
... Mr. Bain told us that Mwini-Chiranga was killed the other day by one of Mwini Msuka's men. The said man visited Chiranga's village and was asking cloth for a wife that was staying there. Chiranga said the woman was merely staying with her mother. The man got rather unruly, and Chiranga gave him a crack across the arm with his club. Whereupon the man thrust two of his spears, one after the other, into Chiranga's belly. Chiranga died shortly afterwards, the man made his escape to some of the Kondi villages, his father, mother, and a friend were caught and put to death, this being native law. When one man does wrong he and all his friends are alike guilty. He (Mr. Bain) also told us that a man was burned to death for witchcraft, he was suspected of being the cause of death of one of Msuku's men. But when Mr. Stewart's dog was killed two years ago by the leopard, it confirmed their ideas and he was caught and tied, and burned with green wood, a most cruel death, but as they say themselves and it is good enough for any person capable of bewitching leopards. We were ignorant of anything like this taking place at the time, it has only now leaked out.
... at 4 pm Mr. Monteith arrived from the lake, he being on his way to Tanganyika with a caravan of goods for the L.M.S. He is in rather an excited state over a lot of stuff

---

[48] The missions and the ALC, *faut de mieux*, found themselves having to administer justice which in one case of execution and floggings, caused an uproar at home.

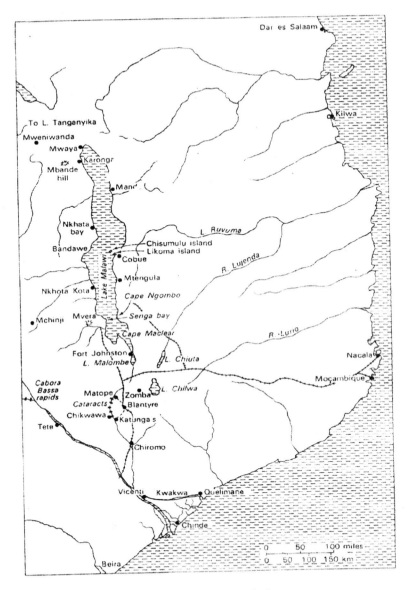

Modern map of East Central Africa

that is lying at Kapakolo for the last 3 or 4 months, as it is rumoured that the robber Chief Chimaraunka, has stolen some of it….. Mr. McEwan and he had some words about calico that Mr. McEwan paid for the company out of the road calico and which was to be paid back in same kind. Mr. Monteith wanted to pay it back with inferior stuff which of course could not be accepted. Also about some beads that Monteith took without liberty from the road store and was going to pay it like all the rest of the calico, etc. by crediting the road with it through the books. This system can never work as the company cannot give supplies, we are at present short of calico, beads, hoes, provisions, etc. all of which has been ordered months ago, and even when the last steamer was down all our stuff was lying at Mandala..... it is most disgusting the kind of work that is carried on in the company. As far as I can see it is greatly in want of proper management.[49]

May 6 *(Kasingula)*

Started to overhaul the boxes, there are two boxes that came from Natal from Mr. McEwan's sister and drinks, etc. The most of the whole of the contents are thoroughly destroyed owing to the tins of sweets having melted and saturated everything else in the boxes. It will be a few pounds loss to us both, as it was a joint affair in ordering it..... We paid Kambomba's sons who came up with us from Kambomba's for the blanket, medicine, etc. We gave them a large red blanket (old) that belonged to Mr. Stewart, also 12 yards of good prints, and a print table cloth, we gave them some iron and quinine made up for the old chief, also a bottle of Vaseline for sores, etc. As a finish up present we gave each of the sons a small mirror for himself. As it was me that giving the presents, I was a little surprised to see the two men's faces beam with delight on receiving the little mirrors, they sprung to their feet, caught my hands and kissed them, I was quite taken aback as I never saw such a scene of gratitude in a black or blacks before. We then gave a few large beads for their wives. They were highly delighted, and before leaving us for home, they said we see now with our eyes that the white man is really great, we have been always told by the Arabs that the white men were poor and hard, but they have been deceiving us. We shall tell all our friends at home what the white men are. And we are coming again to see you, as you have been so kind to us.

May 7

Went to air my clothes boxes, some of them very damp. I also had my cats skins turned out to the sun, and was very sorry to see a number of them destroyed by insects. About midday jaundice began to show itself on my skin. I came in to lay down, when I was seized with the worst fit of ague I have had in the country. My feet and hands got quite? notwithstanding the pile of bedclothes and hot water bottle, the fit shaking continued for near two hours, after which I began to sweat and diarrhoea set in, and then jaundice began to show themselves more prominent. I was then seized with biliousness, and dreadful vomiting. My strength failed me all of a sudden and had to be nursed as a child.

May 8

Diarrhoea still very bad and the vomiting continued. Very weak and restless. Mr. McEwan also in fever, but fought against it so that he might nurse me. He seemed to work himself beyond his strength.

---

[49] There was general agreement on the incompetence of the ALC at this time, but there was also friction between that company, the missions, and indeed those working on the road.

Abstracts from the Diary of William McEwan

22 May - June 25 1884: 'I shall begin to think of returning'

After arrival on April 21 McEwan makes an exploratory trip upriver from the port of Quilimane.

22 May 1884

A short visit up this bank of the river of about 8 miles to visit an opium plantation to see the character of the villages en route but principally to gather information about the river system in this part of the country. And for this I was very well situated in having a Scotchman to go with me who has been resident in the district for some time, as engineer to the opium company. Mr. Henderson has gained a certain amount of notoriety among the people more immediately connected with the ALC. He came out with the original starters, the Moirs, the year I do not know, but some time ago, being discontented with their conduct of business, he left and accepted his present situation. It is well known that he has now received a much larger salary and he has been blamed with degenerating and instead of devoting himself to 'Christian trading', surrendering himself to the temptations of filthy lucre. This blame is perhaps considerably augmented by the fact that Mr. H has taken to himself a kaffir wife, but his conduct has rather brought to the front, at least to my mind, the policy of the ALC regarding salaries.

If I ever reach Maliwanda and have time to commit to paper my ideas on the company in general (supposing it then to be in existence) I shall have something to say on this point. I found Mr. Henderson very similar to the representatives of the ALC I have met here – hospitable, but rather uncultured. (and I venture this criticism at the risk of being called 'uppish'). He gave me plenty of valuable information regarding the different conditions, affluents, connections and overflows about the river system here which I shall embody in a separate report afterwards.

... The journey across to the Zagua is three miles along a path—unusually straight as a whole—running through long grass in the usual way. I did not go to Mopea town as it is some distance higher up the Zagua than the point where the road just touches the river. Having carefully paced the distance between the two rivers I retraced my steps a short distance and turned off to the Opium Planting which occupies an area of 200 acres about the spots marked AA (Sketch). I was too much occupied with making enquiries at Mr. Henderson's to go into an examination of opium manufacture and all I gathered was from walking across the fields. The work is done almost entirely by Kaffirs superintended by coolies who have been brought from India specially to superintend this work—but I hear that the venture has not proved a success and is likely to be withdrawn soon. There are at present about 900 natives employed hoeing and making irrigation channels. The water for this purpose is pumped out of adjacent lakes. The headquarters of the company are built near the Zagua on a raised piece of ground surrounded by a concrete wall, the whole placed at such a height as keeps it out of the water when the adjacent country including the plantations is entirely covered with water, almost an annual occurrence.

I found Mr. Henderson well and lonely and glad to meet someone from Glasgow which he knows well. Being a Stirling man to some extent he was exceedingly pleased to have met Prof. Drummond. That gentleman has left nothing but a good name behind him. Everyone seems to have been delighted with his company and manner both in social and religious matters and it might be better if the people up-country and here too were more permanently treated to the company of such cultured and lucid people as the Professor. At the same time there is an impression that his stay in the country has been too short for his opinion on development and treatment of natives to be valuable. Mr. Henderson seems somewhat exercised as to the correctness of having taken a native wife. It is an almost universal practice among whites in this country excepting employees of the ALC. I gather plenty of valuable information from Mr. Henderson and spent the night at his house coming back to Marua the following afternoon.

... I travelled all the way in *machila* doing the 8.5 miles in about 2 hours. There were four carriers. The most usual method is for two to be at each end of the bamboo, but in this case they had one, and took turns—half an hour at a time. Coming smashing through tall reeds one is made forcibly aware of the infinite amount of insect life that must abound in these grassy plains. Every step revealed beetles—ants—mosquitos—and crawlers of all descriptions into the *machila* and at first I attempted to chuck them out, but one soon grows indifferent to anything short of mosquitoes, biting ants and snakes. Of the last I have only seen one specimen and that a deadly one. It was about 3 feet long and three-quarters in diameter. When I saw it, it was crawling along the verandah rail of Mr. Simpson's house, evidently with the intention of coming in but we soon despatched it and its remains are somewhere in the Zambezi.[50]

...It is only at night sitting with a miserable candle and mosquitos biting your ankles that one thinks of fever or any ills at all. In the freshness of the early morning or the beautiful calm of an evening sunset, only thoughts of beauty and health and satisfaction cross the mind. I can by no means realise that I am working on that great river and seeing all these wonderful and interesting sights that we are accustomed to connect mysteriously with the name of Livingstone. Everything appears to me in a hard and matter of fact way and tomorrow I contemplate going down the Zagua with six niggers—thro' monkeys, alligators, palms, hippopotami with much the same feelings that I would have were I at home and under orders to take the 7am train to Alloa and survey the river to Kincardine.[51] The whole thing surprises me mightily and I must almost expect to see you all round the table at 268 but for mosquitos which keep nag-nag-nagging at my ankles and make me wish to get off upcountry 'where mosquitos cease from troubling and suckers are at rest'.

50 Allan Simpson was on the original Livingstone Zambezi Expedition in 1875.
51 McEwan was here confusing alligators with the fresh-water crocodile.

June 1st. Sunday.

Quilimane - I had intended that this journal of my African experiences should consist of various articles such as the preceding, but after a short trial of it I think the best plan will be to keep a daily note of what I have been after or what I have seen and when letter-writing day comes to write a condensation of my journal and copy the letters in my book. Sunday in Quilimane lacks entirely the spirit and conduct of that day at home. At present a church is being erected but quite a new one and not to take the place of any that had seen its day. The Portuguese, about 300 years at Quilimane and only at their first church.[52] The mail steamer was expected today and she was to bring Capt. Forbes' secretary. He proposes to start for Blantyre at once, and as I am to be his fellow passenger according to present arrangements, I was busy setting my boxes for the road, and in the evening writing up my mail—I have letters finished for Bob and Bill Readman, my Oban bairns, Mr. Stevenson, Wallace Bews, Jeannie and Mother and the folks at home. To Jeannie, I have sent about 28 pages describing Quilimane, the river Zagua and Marua. I hope no one will be any the worse of the dose. Not being at my proper work, I have more time for my pen than will always be the case, and this accounts for the quantity—besides, one must always be doing something in these climates. Sunday thoughts are home thoughts and I am glad to have heard by letter received on May 30 that all are well at home. The horse that is here for the Moirs died today after a short illness and Mr. Shearer is in a bad way about it. Mrs. S. is recovering slowly from her fever and we hope to see her tomorrow. 10pm. and no word of the steamer. That is two days late on a two days journey, so she is evidently detained at Mozambique.

June 2nd. Monday: *McEwan departs for Lake Nyasa*

Up at six getting things arranged for my journey. The *Dunkeld* with Mr. Goodrich arrived at 12.30 but he has so much luggage of his own that it was quite impossible to go in the same boat as intended. I might have been away yesterday or Saturday had I known about this, but now it will be a day or more before another boat can be arranged. Such is African travel even in such a civilised place as Quilimane—24 hours put on to the time table for starting will be about it. Mr. S left about 8 with a fine boat and a large crew and my chances of overtaking him are small but I shall have to put all push into an attempt so as if possible to get his company to Mandala. Mr. S showed me the letters from home especially the one from Mr. Stevenson regarding the railway from Kalunga's to Matope via Mandala and regarding Mr. Stanley General Gordon and Mr. Fort meeting up at some time in Central Africa 'to settle the anti-slavery campaign' rather an ambitious programme and evidently thought of before Gordon's extreme complications at Khartoum were heard of.

---

[52] The Portuguese were very much looked down on by the British for their perceived ineffectiveness as colonialists, but part of the vituperation was against their imposition of duties on all goods travelling up the Zambezi, exacerbated by Protestant prejudice against the Catholic Portuguese.

As to the management of communications from Quilimane to Marua I must say that it is not worth the name. The agents here certainly make a good deal of what they have but there is no well kept fleet of boats for taking passengers and goods and things seem to be left to happy-go-lucky chance a good deal. When I went up the river before starting I had to search out 4 paddles for myself and no 2 were the same. There was no proper helm and the one I got had to be tied on with string and sundry other little matters, showing the general condition of affairs. But I do not want to finish up this day's notes with adverse criticism. The kindness of those at home of sending and letters by N & S Mails makes me very glad and Mother's and John's letters by the *Dunkeld* were very refreshing.

June 3 Tuesday

My writing will now become rather illegible as I am at present being paddled up the Quaqua or Kwakwa river and the motion is not conducive to copper plate calligraphy (when writing is so difficult, I must surely get smaller words) This morning I had a visit

On Kwakwa River, Paddling the Boat

from Mr. Shearer at 5.0am. and I was so sleepy that he looked as if he had been a ghost and effects of this kind are always increased by the use of mosquito curtains. The steamer was to sail at 9.00 o'clock and there was a great deal to do before that hour so I was very willing to assist. It is rather unfortunate that when a steamer is in it would require about six people to do the necessary work to anything like satisfaction and at ordinary time two. A kind of medium has been struck by having three people in the office and while it is hardly to be expected that six people would be paid when their united services are only required at fortnightly intervals the present arrangement entails great discomfort and worry, and unsatisfactory work.

... The original agreement between Mr. Raposa and myself was that I should put in my baggage and start at eleven—then this was changed to twelve. I was on the rampart with my traps at that hour, but the boats did not turn up till 1.30, then when they were loaded it was dinner time and 'no one would think of starting when dinner was ready' and that took till three—then there were forgotten letters to write for Mandala and extra provisions to get and so on, and finally I got clear away with the tinned boxes in the canoe and my own personal baggage in the boat. They are to keep company and I have promised the boys 'backsheesh' if they succeed in overtaking Goodrich. He has two tides start and my crew are good and a little baccy will help them to push along.

My boat is proving much more comfortable than the previous one. She has a large canvas boathouse so that one is not constantly slapping one's ears to kill mosquitos, which on investigation merely turned out to be pieces of grass hanging down. The boat has six paddles, which with the poleman, steersman and myself makes nine. I have 'Victoria' and 'Turk' with me and they take up some room, but they are nice company, especially the former which is getting most affectionate while Turk is getting to have a miserable bark and no grrr for watching. The crew are all Kaffirs—none of them know a bit of English—but I do not fear not getting on with them all right. The experience I gained on my former run up the river is very valuable and I am able to make myself much more comfortable, though I am not so unreasonable to expect to find the trip a whit more enjoyable.

At present we are at anchor close to the shore awaiting the turn of the tide to help us up the river. The men are all asleep under their mats in what seems to be most uncomfortable positions but their musical snores speak otherwise. Our companion canoe is alongside. I am snugly housed inside the canvas house. It has two bays or seats. In the first—the one nearest the bow are two of my boxes, and on the top of them are 'Victoria' and 'Turk' actually in one another's arms. It was their only alternative, as both get on top of the boxes instead of having their lodging on the cold ground and they are good enough friends to chum although it took a good deal of shoving and planning before they got settled. Near them is my hand bag in which I carry my clothes I need in the boat—sleeping suit—singlet—towels—soap and kerchiefs, quinine and saline and some pills, these being the medicines most frequently required unless one is actually ill. On the seat in front of me is my canteen placed there as a stand for my hurricane lamp. I had only candles last time but they are somewhat depressing and now I am writing by the light of a good paraffin flame.

On the seat around me are rice, bread, oranges and rolled up pieces of white calico—a box of biscuits—an earthenware bottle which keeps the water delightfully cool—and my little Etna stove. It is for boiling a pint of water with methylated spirits burnt without wick. Mr. Lindsay at Quilimane kindly gave me his stove which was quite useless to him. The Etna requires much less spirit to boil the water if it is kept out of a wind while burning. I am sitting on my valise which is a most comfortable idea as it is filled with clothes and bedding and while my footstool is box no. 3 my back leans on my cork mattress and round my legs is a fine thick blanket so that one can be perfectly comfortable as they only know how. Hung from aloft is my mosquito curtain and hung round the sides of my canvas house are my waterproof, helmet and gun. Would you were here to see me. The 'you' includes all who would wish to see Willie McEwan again.....

June 5

Yesterday the crew paddled splendidly and we got over nearly the same distance as took me two days last time. The appearance of the banks was on the whole pleasing, though the mud and reeds got very tiresome. We saw any amount of kingfishers and other birds whose names I do not know. At three o'clock we passed Nandira—at the time of my former visit it looked a busy kind of place, though small, but yesterday it was quite deserted. Immediately on leaving Nandira the river narrows down to 100 feet between the banks and a channel of perhaps 60 feet consequently the current runs strong and progress is rather slow. If I have fever on this run it will be owing to these two dogs. They have both been in the Zuagua twice—they persist in sleeping beside me and I have to keep awake to turn them out. They don't appear to like the life.

We anchored last night at a little village and before dawn I managed to get a dinner of tinned beef *a la mode*, Worcester sauce, pepper, salt, tea bread and greengage jam and then I boiled some rice for the dogs—attempted to write up this journal and having failed, got my cork mattress laid on the top of my boxes went to sleep. That was at seven o'clock. At eleven I was rudely awakened by finding myself gradually slipping to windward owing to the tide leaving the boat high and dry, but the crew soon put her to rights again and I slept the rest of the night very well, excepting of course when the dogs had to be turned out.....

This has not been such an enjoyable day's sailing as usual, partly owing to the weather and partly owing to a slight headache which I put down to the two dogs. They won't be content with anything less comfortable than I have myself and need to be taught manners. We are into a shallow part of the river just now where the current runs strong and the principal propelling power is long poles. My crew manage the thing as well as any I have seen on the river. However the shove-shove-shove puts any reading or writing out of the question so I have been lying in the boathouse petting the two dogs to make up for the hard usage of last night—thinking much of all at home and reading all my letters received since 27th February '84 the memorable date on which I left home. They are all so kind and encourage me so much that I would never think of destroying them.

...On my previous visit down the Zagua I paid a visit to the orange trees at Mtema and purchased about 100 at the rate of 1/2 d. per dozen. The natives consume a great many. Excepting on one occasion I have never seen one of them pare the skin off, the custom being to cut it into four or six along the line of the piths with a knife and where the oranges happen to be green this is a very good method. During the day we passed several small villages—Ungambo, Laculoco, Candida, and at 5 o'clock Mutu. At this last place there is a store belonging to a Dutch house and it is the most advanced place between Quilimane and Mopea. We went on till half past five and are now anchored to the bank near a hut belonging to a Banyan. These Banyans are all over the place and one need never be surprised to see one in the most outlandish spots. [53]

June 6

We started this morning at 6 o'clock. I had a miserable night's rest all on account of these dogs and they have rid me of more bad temper than anything else for many years. I wakened to find myself with a worse headache than ever and I spent most of the day on my back feeling decidedly miserable. On occasions like these it takes a great deal of self control to keep from calling yourself a fool for leaving the comforts and affections of home and courting the discomforts of a tropical life. We managed to cover a good distance on our day's sail and anchored at 6 on a little bit of sandy beach. The sunset was most beautiful—no blue about it but a deep emerald, red toning down to a bright saffron with a few green clouds on the horizon. The first half of the day's sailing was through a somewhat stale part of the river—reed banks and scant vegetation. In the afternoon I felt very seedy though not feverish and during the day had three doses of 'saline' which I find very easily taken and effective medicine.

June 7

Very weak all day and at times sick—appetite miserable. After this I will always have a boy with me to cook. It is all very well to depend on the one of the crew if you are able to look after him but I was past that. Took more saline. Arrived at Marindenny at 5.30 pm. got all my luggage carried into grass house—crawled up myself and got to bed at once. I couldn't stand more than three minutes at a time.

June 8

Got *machila* to Marua about 11 o'clock and after seeing Mr. Simpson, got to bed again. Mr. Goodrich had left for Chironge early that morning. I had intended accompanying him but being so ill would have put it out of the question even if I had been on time. I took quinine and saline today and although I have very little fever I am only able to shuffle a few steps and I keep to my bed most of the day.

June 9

Much the same as yesterday all day and in bed most of the day.

June 10

Felt a little stronger this morning so took a long quick walk before breakfast, but it was too much for me and I came back to bed for the rest of the day. Took nice plate of rice and milk for breakfast. Cup of tea at 2—cup of tea at 6. 2 pills at 7 then tucked myself in with mattress and a double blanket below and double blanket and Mr. and Mrs MacGilivray's fine rug and never-to-be-forgotten mosquito net.

June 11

Moving about a little but still weak - 4gms Qu"12.

---

[53]   Banyans were Indian merchants.

June 12

A little stronger today but legs not up to much and cannot walk about much. Today had a flitting from the passenger house where I have been staying to new cattle house which has just been finished. This sounds like a descent in high life but it is really a great change for the better. Larger room—watertight roof more ventilation and more away from the noise that goes on among the huts. Took a pill at bedtime.

June 13

Rose at eight feeling like old times but forced to remember that I wasn't right—might have a better appetite if things were decently cooked but the boy at present here doesn't manage it but Mr. Simpson's reprimand may waken him up. (?) Moved about a little all day—took quinine 4gms at 12—bed at eight.

June 14

Same as yesterday but somewhat sick in the forenoon. In the afternoon went to take some views and got the length of having the slide half in when it jammed and I verbally hit someone and bundled up disgusted. I don't think it is the heat but merely carelessness—but I have just remembered fitting one in all right so I beg the maker's pardon and transfer the blame to the sun. The clouds and sunsets here could only worthily be described by Ruskin. Yesterday the former were very like the skies I have often been amused at in Turner's pictures. Q at 12.[54] Sat a little after dinner reading Whyte's lengthening of the Shorter Catechism—it will be specially interesting to me.

June 15

Rose this morning at half past 6 feeling almost well again and looked at the weather and got a shock that sent me off to bed again. I could only see some 15 yards and all was mist. I rose again at 8 to find a different and cheerier scene—beautiful sunshine and everything fresh and bright and Sunday-like and I have had as enjoyable a Sunday as any I have spent in Africa. Before breakfast, I read at *The Shorter Catechism* a little—the extensions and explanations are very clear and to the point, but there are too many references to other books for a traveller. Mr. Simpson and I had breakfast together at ten, stewed fowls seasoned with saffron-boiled fowl-roast fowl, rice, tea and lots of fresh goat's milk.

... After breakfast we went for a walk down the river bank to the next village and up again. I then got settled down in my hammock for the afternoon with *Robertson's Sermons 3rd seri*es. I have 4 vols which I will prize exceedingly and I am only taking one every Sunday. Today my sermon was on 'the tongue' Jas. III 5.6. Robertson is very heavy on scandal and the sermon might safely be sent to Edmund Yates to while away his hours in prison. He speaks principally of the harm a scandalmonger or even a word dropper does himself—every word spoken is so much strength expended that would have been more usefully spent in work. Then there is the injustice to others and he would have

---

[54] 'Q' or 'Qu.' Refers to quinine which was the only effective way to obviate the symptoms of malaria.

us not look out for the bad in any one but the good and even in enemies let us always pick it out and admire. This is the fine broadness I like about Robertson—it is so refreshing and natural that meeting with intolerance is doubly discouraging and unpleasant.

We had dinner at six—a repetition of breakfast and sat talking till eight and then to bed. I could never settle in a place like this where nothing can be done in the later evening excepting under a mosquito curtain. I lay awake for some time thinking what Mother and the rest would be doing - dear Mother, I hope she will always be kept well and happy. I never knew how much I loved her till I came away.

June 16

Mr. Simpson was going off to Morambala this morning so I got up at seven to help him get ready. The mornings just now are exceedingly cold, the thermometer this morning being as low as 58 degrees which is rather unusual. It is very refreshing knocking about in these bright sunny mornings before anything like heat has appeared on the scene. We had breakfast together and shortly afterwards I saw Mr. S. go off. Considering that I was unable to go on he is taking advantage of my being here to go to Morambala and perhaps Chironge to see about the goods of the Af. L. Co. which are lying at a very insecure position at both of these places. He expects to be away for a fortnight and for that time I will remain here to recover and keep a watchful eye on the establishment. There is not a native knows a word of English and I don't know more than a few of their words.

After Mr. S. had gone I came up to my house and rummaged my boxes for nothing—always a cure for loneliness for in them I can always see Mother, Mary and sometimes other people too. Then I opened Jeannie's box of provisions and my mouth watered at the 'Pine Apple Chips' that are only to be opened at Maliwanda - would I were there. *McEwan refers to reading some of his much admired Ruskin and finding some of Longfellow's poems – an indication of his serious library, but with a miserable night with rats running up and down his mosquito net.*

June

Had cup of tea in bed at seven and rose shortly after. It is stale, flat and unprofitable not having any set work to do—rising morning after morning to wonder what I will do today. 'Idleness is undoubtedly chief of vices all' and I make a point of always being after something. Today I put up my tent and flier complete. It looks A1 and everything is shipshape. I could always put it up with the help of two men—two blockheads would do. I also got all my boxes weighed and not one but was considerably overweight which means another day among them to try and get them right before starting from here.[55] I had a cup of tea and biscuit at two and dinner at 6 consisting of stewed fowl with lots of gravy and rice and rice and milk and a chapter of Green's *History* and after taking some plates out of the slides got to bed at 8. I had flitted to the tent to escape mosquitos and rats but these evils were only mitigated and I had only an indifferent night's rest.

---

[55] The average weight carried by porters, usually as headloads were about 60lbs, but with their own belongings could be as much as 80lbs.

1 June

Time goes like electricity here and it is always Wednesday when I think it is but Tuesday or Saturday instead of Friday and as long as I am not at my work or on the way to it this remains so. James's birthday.[56] I have been thinking of his desire to come out here too. I fear he would not be able to keep from working too hard for the climate. It has been a comfort for me the knowledge that he is at home because I know that he will see that mother and Mary will lack nothing.

... afterwards I was busy for some time paying the crews of canoes for Chironge. Each canoe has eight men who get 6 fathoms of white calico each and the hire of the canoe is eight and a half fathoms. Then goods came over from Quilimane which had to be carried over from Marindenny—and I had to pay some men for that—2 yards for a full load and less for smaller loads according to their size and weight. The latter is the ruling feature ...

While sitting in my house reading I saw a strange native go past into the yard. He saluted me and went on and about half an hour afterwards – a deal of loud talk having gone on in the meantime—I met him coming away followed evidently unwillingly by one of the women belonging to the station. He was evidently a slave dealer come after an old slave. I told the women as well as I could by signs that she was free to go or stay and as she elected to go back to the station and showed her choice by scuttling back double quick time, I sent the man about his business and he went without the least humbug but muttering something about shooting somebody.[57] I am rather at a disadvantage here not knowing the language ...

The sunset tonight was bright and deep red gold as usual and purple. Morambala in the distance looked grand and calm. When it got dark which is about 5.45 just now, I got a nice wood fire lit in my house and my lamp nicely trimmed and I am now sitting very cosily before the logs. Before writing this I got through another chapter of Green and also a little of Thomas a Kempis. The religion which he would have us practise is a little to the exclusive side but books like his are a treasure where one is so often solitary. I get stronger every day thanks very much to the plentiful supply of good fresh milk. I take 5 gms of Quinine every day at twelve as a safeguard. The only way I have yet practised in taking it and likely to remain the only way, is wrapping it in a small piece of cigarette paper and washing it over like a pill. I haven't even tasted the Quinine yet. I am just going to watch my fire die out and then go to my tent to bed by which time it will be nine o'clock and the dear folks at home will be just be finishing their tea in good Scotch daylight. May they and I be kept happy and well till we meet again.

---

[56] One of McEwan's brothers.

[57] Despite the formal ending of the slave trade within the Sultan of Zanzibar's dominions as a result of British pressure, it was rampant in the interior, with Nyasaland in particular suffering constant depredations.

June 19

... I am sitting in my house writing by the flicker of a candle the oil in my lamp having gone done. If the foolish virgins had depended on the African Lakes Co. for their supply I think it would have been a valid excuse for their supply running short at the critical moment. It is rather chilly tonight even under the cover and I am glad to have the cheery wood fire burning on the floor beside me. Outside I can hear the men discussing round their fires and away at Mazaro about a mile distant I can hear the most unmusical rum-tum of the native drum. I have just written up my observation calculation book the resulting latitudes ... I have not had an idle day by any means.[58]

... After breakfast, loads began to come from Marindenny and I received about a hundred in all and paid the carriers—that itself means some time. Some of the natives are dreadful sneaks and I had to send one wicked old man to the bottom of the row as I caught him shuffling his load nearer the top to get paid sooner. I calculated some of my later observations—found time to re-read my Sunday's sermon and a bit of Thos. a Kempis and I am now going to have my nightly chapter out of Green and then to bed. Took no Quinine today.

June 20

... I had a note from Simpson today per the boat which had taken up Goodrich which was returning with letters from that gentleman for the home mail when Simpson met it. He says 'Even if you had gone on you would have been stuck up at Chironge so just comfort yourself.' Certainly all this time I am gaining a unique experience but it is not in connection with my work and it is doing little or no good and if there is a probability of much further delay I shall begin to think of returning and getting on with my studies without losing more time hanging on here. Nearly a quarter of my engaged time gone without my seeing the scene of my labours is past a joke. I have to be thankful for the good health I have enjoyed in a district with such a bad name and at this season immediately after the rains which is considered the worst and I only hope it augurs an ability of suitability of constitution for African travel ...

June 21

The end of another week still finds me at Maruru and in the meantime in charge of the station. In health I am almost myself again, though I doubt if my legs would carry me 16 miles a day. That was where the fever affected me most and it was very humiliating to be barely able to walk. I never was so weak in my life before and it was a very funny experience. My appetite is now making up for what it lost then and I fare sumptuously every day on stewed fowl, rice and goat's milk—indeed today I think I ate too much ...

Rose at 7 and devoted the day to photography - took three views in all and developed them but not very successfully. My darkroom consisted of blankets sewed together and hung over the table, but it was too dark and I could not follow the developing and had just to keep the developer moving till I thought the plate was developed and then mash it

---

[58] McEwan had his important astronomical observations and latitudes/longitudes published in the Proceedings of the Royal Geographical Society.

and put it in the alum and hypo baths. The vulcanate dishes I have two raised lines running longitudinally which allow the developer to run in below the plate and correspondingly more is needed to go over the film side. I found the plates difficult to cover all over and my first view was spoilt owing to my not managing this properly. However I am encouraged to proceed as my results are not bad for a first attempt of one who isn't even an amateur.

June 22

My Sundays in Africa promise to be bright spots judging from my experience of today and last Sunday. I will now look forward to them for their quiet rest and solitude giving me more time and opportunity and inclination than the bustle and companionship of home life would admit for thinking on and studying the deeper things of life. I rose at 6.30 and before breakfast had a short walk and read my weekly sermon from F.W. Robertson. His subject was 'The Victory of Faith' 1John v.4-5 I think it says much for the worth of these sermons, that while prepared for and preached to civilised congregations in Brighton, I can still find in them much that is helpful, instructive and encouraging towards trying to do one's duty, having found it out, and to do it well ...

June 23

McEwan spends much of the day making prints from negatives and lists the photos he has taken, mainly of his immediate surroundings. He refers to one of Mr. Simpson's house with living quarters on the second floor with the comment 'to be high is to be healthy' i.e. the misconception that malaria came from the ground and one of the reasons why travellers would sometimes avoid moving when there was early morning mist low down.

I idled a good deal of yesterday afternoon and could stick at nothing which—paradoxical as it may seem—means that I stuck at everything. However I always have the comfort of a large appetite and lots to appease it. I read the introduction to Robertson's life and looked at an algebra and walked down to the river and so on. I had just finished tea and was arranging my tent and my mosquito curtains and my light to try and get some reading done there when the 'Capitao' came in to tell me that a *Mzungu* [59] had arrived so I turned out and found Mr. Deuss (pronounced Doyce) a German on his way from Quilimane to Inhamissago wanting a night's lodging which of course he got. I had to get him a bed and see his house right and get something cooked for him which woke me up completely and over the meal he told me he had come as far as Mutu with a Mr. Millar a former employee of the A.L.C. returned to their service ...

... It was 10 o'clock when I saw Mr. Deuss housed for the night and when I got to my tent there was Victoria snoozing on my bed with her two forepaws (of course it couldn't be her three) sticking through my mosquito curtain—two lovely rents. I immediately sent for a strap and thrashed her so that she didn't turn up all night and as Turk happened to

---

[59] *Mzungu* is a European or white person.

see the chastisement he thought he had better be going too and I saw nothing of either till morning and had a fine night's rest.

June 24

I am writing now at 4.pm after a busy day of it. There was first Mr. Deuss to see away, but that was no trouble—on the contrary he greatly assisted me—being up in the language in giving orders to send a *machila* to Marindenny for Mr. Millar. Then as he was to be so late in arriving and had the mails I gave up hopes of getting my letters before sending off the Quilimane canoe with the home mail. The men did not turn up soon and I had to send out to hurry them up then first half an hour after I had got them despatched a boy arrived with an up country mail and I hurried to run through it—take out Simpson's letters and send it post haste after the canoe men and I am glad to say the messenger overtook them all right. The news from up-country is important. Steamer re-working, F. Moir at Chironge, Mrs. Moir had a daughter followed by a most dangerous fever. I expected at Morambala on steamer's next run. If Mr. Millar is agreeable to stay here till Simpson's return I will pack up and go off at once ...

June 25

Rose at 6.30 a pleasant fresh morning and not too cold. This was about the most idle day I have spent here knocking about all day settling to nothing and living in constant expectation of Millar's arrival with the home mails.[60] His loads were coming up in two's and three's but he didn't turn up until 5.30. I understand that when in the country before some four years ago he was known as 'Wee' Millar'—quite a fair description.

He has an indifferent crew and consequently had rather a lengthy journey. We had dinner at once and I gave him all the news I had from up-country. He agreed at once to stay at Maruru and allow me to go on so I will have a day of it tomorrow getting off. He brought me letters from Mother at King's Road—Jeanie, Mary and Robert—Mrs MacDonald and Buchanan at Hope Street. The mosquitos were all on the move so I read them all after getting into bed. Jeanie has sent me two bundles of newspapers per the steamer box which Millar had seen at Quilimane but which were not forwarded. If there is anything I will not tolerate while in this country it is neglect of mails. I have said nothing this time leaving Millar to remind them to send them on ...

---

[60] Millar was one of the many artisans—sailors, engineers, weavers, craftsmen, *et al*— mainly recruited from the west of Scotland by the Livingstonia Mission and the ALC.

June 26 to August 31 1884: A reconnaissance north

Karonga Station

McEwan leaves the ALC station at Maruru on a reconnaissance as far as the proposed main road station at Maliwanda, before returning to the depot at Karonga.

June 26 Maruru

Rose at 6.15 and commenced arranging and locking up boxes for my journey. I had first to send out the Capitao to get paddles for the boat—meantime I worked away first getting my photo box put right. It is wonderful how long it takes to put back the things one has been using for a week. There is always some little thing to come out and gradually boxes get half emptied. It took me till two o'clock to get everything ready—tent packed, etc. etc. Then I have to pay 10 men—100 yards of calico in all—and then they went off for their goods and mats. Millar has brought up word that the mail going south would be a week late so I was able to send short notes to Mother and Durban telling them I was in for another stage of my prolonged journey.

In the end I got off at 5.15 with a good cargo of luggage including 4 boxes for Mrs. Moir's baby and keg of ?, 11 sacks of flour, mails for Mandala, Nyasa and Maliwanda. I have a fine large boat—the best I have had on my travels yet. Wooden house about 8 feet long and comfortable in height. I am getting quite an experienced hand at making myself comfortable ...

... Large quantities of duckweed came floating down the river from Morambala marsh. We stopped for the night at a place on the ? bank about 200 yards below 'Vianno'. I had visited Vianno when at Mopea some time ago and as he was a kind of civlised half-caste, thought I might get some bread there. On going up I found Vianno was away but I asked for 'pow' the Portuguese for bread and after waiting two minutes they brought me a bundle of firewood, about the nearest approximation to asking for bread and getting a stone I know of ...

June 27

... the salmon rice dish was not so palatable as I expected and awoke tender recollections of Mary's fine salmon cakes ... I was told that the place was occupied by a tribe called Landeens who were dead enemies of the Portuguese one of whom at one time had killed some of the Landeens in an underhand way. Mr. S also said that English were pretty safe to land tho' the Landeens might come down and take possession of the boat. It was acting on this information that I got out my photo apparatus, intending to photograph Mrs. L's grave, pocketed my revolver with some spare cartridges and instructed the captain to wait by the boat and allow no one in. As we drew near to Chupanga I could see a great crowd of men moving about and I began to think 'Well, here's a go—a pretty appearance for a place said to be inhabited by a few Landeens. As I got nearer, I could see that they were engaged in some sort of earthwork or other and then when my eye lighted on the Portuguese flag, I knew 'things are not as you are told' so I ran the boat up on the bank and went ashore with two of the crew. It was rather a lively sight—two or three hundred natives and one group with Turkish fezzes and armed.

They received me with a simultaneous clap of the hands which was rather alarming and then I walked up to the house. The ground slopes gradually up from the river about 1 in 25 and there is a straight road up to the house which is 150 yards from the bank. The place is a little ruined and out of repair but in going in the sight of one large gun and two small ones, mounted on wheels, revealed to me at once what was up. The Portuguese are building a small fort with which to overawe the Landeens and take possession of the right bank of the Zambezi from which they have so often been repulsed. Unfortunately having erected a fort and formed a military establishment at a place their efforts stop there and I dare say Chupanga will become like other of their stations—a place to sink money and men—military—and perhaps some years after this to be occupied and developed by representatives of other nations ... The Commandant of the place received me most graciously and I was much surprised here to find the manager of the Mopea Opium Co whom I had met while visiting Mr. Henderson. Mrs. Livingstone's grave is just a little to the east of the fort (under the well-known baobab tree and will be outside of it when the works are finished ... Away due north was the Morambala range – the one thing the eye always turns to here—looking clearer in the evening light than it had been all day and looking for all the world like Arran as seen from Wemyss Bay on the arrival of the 4.35 on a fine summer afternoon; only of course it is the only hill and the high peak is to the left instead of nearer the centre.

June 29

... I thought I heard rats during my snooze and my suspicions were forcibly confirmed in the morning by finding the back part of my pith helmet nibbled in several places. This is the more aggravating as it cost 15/- and is my only one ... the crew had not escaped as the rats had tackled their fish ... In the afternoon I began a long letter to Mrs MacDonald ... 'Turk' and 'Victoria' are getting very affectionate—the former licking Vic's sore ears and her wet feet.

June 30

This is the most unsundaylike Sunday I have spent since leaving home as far as appropriate feelings were concerned. It was a wet miserable day, bleak and ? like and I have not sufficient what may be called 'spiritual depth' to be independent of surroundings in my feelings, either sacred or secular. In connection with the question of not travelling on Sunday I know that to have stopped on a day like this would have produced anything but devotional feelings. *(In the event McE was in error - it was a Monday so he need not have worried)* ... I felt that on entering the Shire another stage of my journey was over slow as it is.

July 1

McE refers to meeting up just in time with the steamer by 'holleering' just as she was about to leave and meets up with Simpson and Gowk who had been captured by the Makololo along with the steamer ... he passed a very anxious time but was allowed to live as usual on the steamer under a guard. The steamer has been recovered with the consent of the head chief Kasisi but Chikusi and another man objects and things are sufficiently shaky to make us be careful about arms going up the river. The three of us had dinner together and anyone seeing us wouldn't have imagined but that we were three chaps from some healthy glen in the highlands with corresponding appetites.

July 2

... After getting clear of Marambala, the edges of the river begin to grow marshy and by a gradual process we are led into the great Marambala Marsh. At this time in the present condition of the river, it appeared more as an immense lake stretching many miles in all directions ... on today's journey, I have seen more alligators and different kinds of birds since leaving Quilimane.

July 5

... At six o'clock a note came in from Morrison from four miles off and his men soon began to come in with their loads, he following about eight o'clock - a big built fellow looking something like a wild man of the woods with long uncut hair and a scraggy beard. He had been quite successful on his journey and got all he wanted—likes the life immensely and it seems outwardly to suit his constitution. [61]

---

[61] Morrison was an engineer on the *Ilala*, the first steamboat to be put on Lake Nyasa, after being brought up the Shire and carried in sections round the Murchison cataracts.

July 6

These last two Sundays have not increased my sympathy with people who always stop travelling on Sundays, in Africa. Anchored to a bank with the villagers sitting in a row, looking at you all day and gabbling like parrots all the time spoils a Sunday for me. We ate, read a little and talked most of the day without much mutual benefit to health and intellect and turned in early.

July 7

When the steamer was released the matter could not be considered then settled and on today's journey we encountered the present position of affairs in its various aspects. For my information on this matter I am chiefly indebted to Mr. Morrison. When Livingstone left the Shire country, some of his Makololo men remained behind and gradually took a position among the natives in various places taking the place of chiefs. Two of these were Kasisi or Ramakukan and Mloka. They were united in a bond of eternal friendship and were as one, Mloka being the nominal superior. He had as attendant a boy named Chipitula who on the death of Mloka many years ago rebelled against Kasisi who then became chief and set up on his own account in that district where we are now. (Mloka's son at present being chief under Kasisi) Chipitula was a successful rebel and acquired a power with which Kasisi could not have coped and consequently he gradually came to be a recognised chief and all remembrances of his being a rebel were forgotten. He was a cruel tyrant among his own people often killing them with his own hand but at all times he was the friend of the white man and it was always his great desire to have a white wife.

His heir Chikusi was at one time at Blantyre school but turning out a regular 'bad un' he was expelled. He was a mere boy, but on Chipitula being shot by Fenwick, Chikula was duly installed as his successor.[62] Why Kasisi did not at such an opportune moment assert his supremacy and appoint another successor—perhaps Nloka's son—I know not. Chikusi being a regular 'bad un' at school has not improved now and he and a few of his men want to make capital out of Chip's death but Kasisi says that all the other under chiefs in the villages which belonged to Chip are for peace. Chikusi himself is afraid of Kasisi and I cannot understand why the latter doesn't put down his foot especially with the English behind him. Today, shortly after leaving Mpatsa we came to a village on the right bank where Kasisi was staying and he came on board and had a chat and some dinner—the first time I have seen a black eating in civilised fashion.

... this is one of the places where firewood is cut for the steamer and the place where Gowk was captured. When on their way down Chikusi had sold firewood but when we landed he sent word we would not get it which was rather awkward. Morrison talked to Philip—the boy who wrote the deceptive letter to Gowk and he said that he was sorry for

---

[62]   This was the notorious incident when one of the artisans, Fenwick, in a drunken rage, shot and killed the local chief and was in turn speared to death by his vengeful Makololo tribesmen. (see Munro diary for fuller description) Fenwick's widow married another missionary, the Rev. Alexander Hetherwick.

having deceived the English—bunkum I daresay. There were not many of Chikusi's men about, but those on the bank were excited and while Morrison and Gowk were in the village, talked and gesticulated at a great rate, the boys on the steamer telling us afterwards that they said they wouldn't take the steamer this time but when it came down next run they would take it and Gowk would hold a big *mirandu* which is the name they give to their big councils. There is one at present in progress with reference to the whole business.

One man was more prominent in his excitement than the rest and was always being restrained by another who we learned afterwards was an old Livingstonia boy. When coming away even the children were lively a bit and the people cried after us if we were going away with the steamer again. One of Kasisi's men was coming on board when some of Chikusi's men tore off his cloth and we left him there trying to recover it. If he happens to be a big man of Kasisi's and doesn't recover his fathom of dirty calico there may be a row. Ultimately we got away quite safely somewhat relieved but rather in a fix for want of the firewood as there was only a four or five hours supply on board.

July 10
Today was rather warm and in the small aftercabin of the *Lady Nyassa* was almost unbearable ... Capt. Foot the Nyasa Consul happened to be there (at Katunga's) being on a short journey visiting some chiefs ... at Katunga's there is a large grass store and house belonging to the company.

July 11
... I was wakened by a Blantyre boy who had been sent on with Mr. F. Moir's donkey to take me the rest of the way which is said to be 12 miles, a distance I would hardly have managed without another 2 hours sleep in the middle. However I was decidedly grateful to see the animal and was not long in getting on its back I soon passed all the men and got into Mandala at six while it was still daylight. These 12 miles are the most level part of the road ... I soon had tea with Mr. and Mrs Moir and Mr. F and spent the evening discussing the road. Mr. F was going off in the morning and I had to get his views.[63] What we agreed was that where the work was in anyway difficult the width should be restricted to 7 feet. That a new road be made for the first 10 miles from Lake over plain practically a clearance—that the south side of the? Hills be taken for routes—I received many hints that the terminus be at ... on Lake Tanganyika there being no bad descent as reported that being only North two points many miles apart the crest along which is quite accessible. For routes from Mambwe to the Lake Mr. F.M. gave me all his information and said Zombe was out of position on all maps.

July 15
In the forenoon I had a visit from Consul O'Neill[64] who came to return Ravenstein's letter about the longitude of Blantyre which I had sent him.[65] He of course is interested in

63   'Mr F'. and 'F.M'. refers to Fred Moir, brother of John.
64   Henry O'Neill had been a naval officer at Zanzibar.

observation and we had a short chat ... O'Neill has fixed Blantyre by a long series of lunars so I will do nothing here. After tea I had a spell at Mr. Moir's harmonium and to bed at ten.

July 17

... one of the herd boys came in to say that he had seen a lion prowling about near the cattle. This is an unusual occurrence so Mr. Moir sent him off and told him to come back if he saw anything. He returned in about three quarters of an hour so we got up a party and went on the hunt but were unsuccessful. Mr. Munro saw the lion, but I was not so fortunate ... The afternoon was spent promiscuously as usual and Munro came up to my house at night. Everyone is greatly delighted with my photos, especially the two young ladies.

July 19

I spent part of this forenoon in going over one of Mr. Stewart's boxes containing a number of papers relating to the road ... Munro came in a great hurry to say that the lions had turned up again and had killed some goats so off we went again—a big party but without getting them. Munro saw one but couldn't manage a shot. There were no less than 4 dead goats lying about so Mr. Moir poisoned one in the hope of getting the marauders that way. In the afternoon I had a read at Livingstones's *Zambezi*. About six o'clock it was discovered that the two donkeys had not been in for the night and as they had been seen up the road where the lions were, Mr. Moir was in a great state and he and Mr. Munro started off with a few boys in search and turned up about 8 o'clock unsuccessful.[66] Meanwhile Mrs Moir had grown tired of waiting and we had tea together. When the searchers came in they had tea and then a large gang was organised to go out with lamps. Lion hunting is passable but donkey hunting—never—so when the party went off I turned into my cottage.

July 23

Mr. M has kindly lent me a specimen gun for shooting small birds. In the evening Munro and I were busy filling cartridge cases, making bullets.

July 25

Wrote out list of provisions, ammunition, etc purchased from the Co. for road and self. After breakfast photo'd baby Moir.

July 26

McE refers to Mr. Stewart's letters to Rev. Thomas Main in Scotland from Livingstonia in 1879 suggesting Bandawe as a suitable harbour--also to Mr. Stevenson from Karonga July 1883 referring to meeting with chiefs and good description of the topography in the district of Maliwanda.

---

[65]   E.G. Ravenstein was an assiduous geographer and mapmaker.

[66]   Munro gives a fuller description of this incident in his diary.

Ilala at Matope

July 28

The *Ilala* mail arrived about mid-day. She had experienced real stormy weather and requires a week to repair. Bain and all the others are well although he has been sadly bothered by a want of calico. The only passenger was Captain Hore who arrived in the afternoon rather footsore having given his walking shoes to Bell—a hunter on the lake—and walking from Matope till the donkey met him in canvas shoes.[67] He seems to know Tanganyika, its surroundings and peoples well and I am extremely glad to see him coming down by this route. He will probably be dissatisfied with it in its present state of working which may best be described as congested, but his coming seems to betoken a firm friendship between the LMS and those to the southward. He gave us some account of the state of affairs on Tanganyika in relation to Arab civilisation and the treatment of natives. He has written a memorandum on the road for my benefit in case of not seeing me and I anticipate in getting it to complete my gathering of advice and information and to be able to go on with the road.

Hore's idea of the working of the missions on Tanganyika is to have a chain of shore stations and then when ways and means permit a parallel series in the heights which surround Tanganyika. In accordance with this his directors at present declined to form a station on the road except near the terminus. However we still have to discuss the matter fully and it was only an occasional conversation that we interchanged views tonight.

---

[67] A former navyman, Capt. Edward C. Hore was in charge of the London Missionary Society (LMS) project on Lake Tanganyika. The LMS received financial support from Stevenson in exchange for agreeing to use the Zambezi route for transport and for agreeing to establish a station at the south end of Lake Tanganyika on the line of the Stevenson Road. (see also Munro's comments).

July 29
... Spent the afternoon writing and making a copy of a letter which Mr. Hore has written to me regarding the road, etc. He has taken great pains to give me all the information he possesses and has taken a lot of trouble in preparing for me a sketch of his route with the striking features near at hand which will certainly be of use to me. After tea, Mr. Moir, he and I had some conversation regarding the Tanganyika end of the road. Mr. Hore has written his directors recommending Niumkolo on the shore at the south end of Tanganyika as a good site for their station. It was always the intention of the ALC to have a station at the terminus of the road on Tanganyika and Niamkolo seems the only suitable terminus so that the intentions of the two bodies may clash. Mr. Hore thinks there would be objections to both parties working at the same place but says it is a matter for discussion at home. He also anticipates that if the ALC plant a station on Tanganyika and endeavour to direct to Nyasa the ivory that at present proceeds eastwards by the Unyanyembe route a big *mirandu*[68] of the Arabs will be held and difficulties may arise.

August 7
Sailing on the Shire and on Lake Nyasa. We started about 6.30 and about 9.45 entered the Lake and Livingstonia about 3.30. Sailing NW along the shore towards Cape Maclear is quite like the coast of Natal. Livingstonia, excluding the hills, immediately suggests Delagoa Bay.

August 8
This forenoon I went through three of Mr. Stewarts boxes that were lying at Livingstonia and took away some papers relating to the road ... The *Ilala* is a beastly little boat with a beastly little cabin. She was very suitable for what she was built i.e. a mission boat but when she is loaded up with goods everything gets dirty and uncomfortable very soon and neither Harkness or Fredericks - the men on board seem to have any idea of things being in order.

August 10
... spent most of the day meditating on things in general and the home folks in par-ticular—not home-sick—but finding more and more how I loved all, but still exceedingly glad to be on my way up. But these Sundays in travel are not enjoyable and my sermon from Robertson did me no good. The whole feeding on the *Ilala* up till now has been roast fowls wretchedly cooked with the gravy stolen, half cleaned red rice, tea, bread, butter and jam. Here the inhabitants have bowed more to the rough life than any I have yet met and little attempt is made at cleanliness and comfort. A little steamer crammed with goods is hardly the place for much of this but I would manage a little more style.

---

[68]   *Mirandu/mlandu* is a meeting to decide a case.

August 11

... The people at Bandawe when we arrived were Dr. Scott and Mrs Scott and master Scott, a baby boy still in his cradle. Mr. Smith, teacher and most experienced man on the mission Mr. McCallum a joiner or something of the country and one of those artisans likely to cause trouble and a Mr. Nicol who had been buying ivory for the Co. from the Angoni on the hills. The mission work of course we saw nothing of and when the steamer arrives with the mails the secular work is somewhat disorganised. Mr. Hore at Mandala expressed great satisfaction with Mr. Smith's school and saw in it great hopes for the future but scholars were on holiday while I was there and I was disappointed of the sight. Dr. Scott does some dispensary work, but I daresay the natives will 'take the loan' of medical kindness if not strictly watched ...

One of the great objections to the place is its bad anchorage there being only the barest shelter. Mr. Stewart's note of the place as to harbourage the place where he suggested a breakwater being at C on the sketch. The adjacent hill is composed almost entirely of stones and with proper appliances the work is quite possible but there must be none of that working without efficient means which is killing much good work here and which is traceable in most cases to want of management on the part of the Coy—want of carrying power, lack of which are in part traceable to the action of the home representatives of the company. I have not taken any pains to correct or add to the geography of the Lake, and I am reserving myself, as it were, for my own sphere, my own home to be, between Nyasa and Tanganyika and if I have strength given to do my work properly, I do not fear desertion of my ever-present guide.

McE then refers to the South African missionary Mr. William Koyi and his work with the warlike Angoni in the hills who sometimes descend to attack - the locals live in constant dread of them.

August 12

... I propose confining any study I may manage in this country to mathematics and the language—Chinyanja first and Swahili if possible.

August 14

... one of the boys drew my attention to 'Nyama-Nyama' and I managed to make out a herd of zebras grazing among the trees about 120 yards off. I stalked them to 70 yards when off they went running diagonally across my front and I took a flying shot with my Snider and brought down one of the herd. It was coming near dinner time so I went no further and after the first death natives get slightly excited. They call all eating game 'Nyama' and it is a great luxury for them. They make a night of it usually and they slept on shore and made a regular night of it.

August 15

McE refers to landing from the Ilala at Karonga - refers to Mr. Monteith being there as the Company's agent who had been trading in ivory a little ... but he grumbles much at not being supplied with sufficient cloth either for trading or for taking a caravan to LMS steamer to Tanganyika which is now the enterprise devolving on him.

August 16 Karonga

... on getting up this morning I found that the rats had a feed off my helmet. The place seemed overrun and they attack everything without respect.

August 17

... Mr. Nicol and I walked out to the Baobab tree where Mr. Stewart and Captain Gowans are buried. Munro has put up a nice little railing round the graves and carved a cross on the tree but the growth is very thick and would need constant cleaning. The chief has been paid a certain amount of cloth and the enclosed ground is considered the property of the English and is respected by the natives. The graves are about a mile from Karonga House and winding through the native houses and through the banana groves ... I am inclined to have places occupied by whites called by English names as has been done at the Congo and at Blantyre or at any rate by native names distinct from those of the chief as 'Mandala', but all the people who have been any time in the country to whom I have spoken on the subject prefer sticking entirely to the native names.

August 18

Getting ready to start for Maliwanda, McE speaks of his stores and preparations—refers to constant wearing of flannel belts day and night as a preventative against chill when falling asleep without blankets properly covering him. A tin containing chlorodyne pills. sticking plaster. A little bit of cotton, and of oil silk and a bottle of saline. - the brandy flask has a corner also. For books I have packed the nautical Almanac 1884, Star Atlas revised Version, Hints to Travellers, Notebooks, etc. and I have taken the following instruments - 6" sextant, artificial horizon, Abney's level, prismatic compass, two 2 and half inch aneroids, thermometer. For sport and protection—shotgun, snider rifle, revolver and lots of ammunition ... while sorting up we came on one of Mr. Stewart's boxes which I eagerly explored for any trace of the remaining geographical instruments that are to fall to me and was delighted to find the large-sized prismatic compass that no one knew anything about. It was very aggravating to find after the steamer had left as the stand is at Bandawe and I was anxious to get it up. This is a lesson to make sure for oneself: I had accepted Monteith's assurance that all Stewart's instruments were at Maliwanda.

August 19

McE gives names of his porters including one who had survived the massacre in Stewart's time ... though we now had the refreshing hills round about us on the road still persevered along the plain and not very far from the Rukuru which runs almost parallel for some distance. At a quarter to one we were opposite Karamba's village where there is the first attempt at earthwork, then there is about a mile of ordinary road round a plain and then we enter upon what Mr. Stewart always considered to be the most difficult part of the road. And truly the work that has been done astonished me and considering the means the end is surprising. It reminded me very much of the cuttings along Loch Awe on the C & O Railway and the formation of ground that had to be faced is very similar. Steep hills coming right down to the water's edge ... many landslips have taken place and considerable work will have to be put forth to make the road right but this is no detraction from a road made with unskilled labour and also a road <u>not maintained</u>.

Even on this the first day's journey the scenery is more enjoyable than any I have yet seen in Africa and it is the greatest possible pleasure for me to be at work and I am thankful to feel well ... came back to dinner at four and found any amount of natives ·with provisions - sweet potatoes, fowls, eggs, and of these I purchased some fowls at a foot of prints and eggs at ten for a foot and then I sent for some milk and got it as sour as before ... deep thankfulness for the kindness which allows me to be here at my work and hoping that all those I love so well are happy and comfortable at home. Distance today about 17 m.

August 20

... the road has been constructed on a pleasant gradient *round* the hill but owing to some slips it is at present quite impassable. We have had many examples today of the inability of the natives to take advantage of the fact that the distance round a bucket handle is the same whether it be vertical or lying flat. Where the path runs near a winding stream, they persist in cutting off the bends by a straight path which of course entails a steep ascent and descent while a path round by the edge of the stream would be about the same length and nearly level ... when we left the plain, the next part of the road was a long gradual ascent to the higher hills. The work done is very good, but the surface is left very rough and some immense boulders which block the way would require blasting ... at 8.15 we came to the end of the road constructed near here ...

The route at this place had not been settled by Mr. Stewart and I have seen sufficient difficulties today to make me wish to survey the country a little more and traverse the alternative route which according to Munro is two miles longer and passes near a village called Mwini Chiranga ... We stopped at this camping place on the banks of the Lufira R. at 4.15 having travelled not less than 20 miles and my Wellingtons have raised a nice compound blister on my right heel. It always goes first and I was as pleased as the men to get into quarters. Dined on one of Norton's 'Mutton Broth' boiled rice with eggs beat in and tea with beat eggs, biscuits and jam. Where eggs are 1" of cloth at 8 per yard each I don't think it is extravagant to use so many especially when there is no milk. Of course I have been in Oban in spirit and gone in for raffles in spirit (the safest plan) and assisted at the opening of the bazaar.[69] I hope all are well and that everything will go off satisfactorily.

August 21

... Mr. Stewart seems to have stuck to the native path very consistently and little bits of the road being constructed here and there on that principle and so there will be no use trying to find a better route, the only work being to connect these detached portions ... Even in my tent I am reclining on my truss of calico, clothed in the big ulster nursing my

---

[69] Previously McEwan had referred to 'his bairns' (possibly nephews or nieces) in Oban but there is otherwise no obvious connection with this Scottish town.

poor heel and trying to make a few truthful notes about my journey ... I expect to reach Maliwanda in time to breakfast with Mr. Bain.

August 22

... That part of the road which we traversed this morning is laid out in long straight lines (joined with curves which could almost be called angles) through wood and over grassy flats which show signs of being rather moist in the rainy season. Near Maliwandas, the road is laid out through the native gardens and some parts seem to have been left unmade until the crops were cleared. The growth is in many places very heavy consisting of young trees but from end to end I have seen no tree growth that two blows of an axe would not clear and no grassy growth that the native hoe cannot tackle easily. We passed over the 'village green' where a *mirandu* or conference was in progress at which Maliwanda himself was present so of course he came forward to scrutinise my little caravan and Pemba told him where I was bound for. He is a big chief physically whatsoever be his other claims to rank—rather more than 6' 2ins and topped with a rather loosely knitted tam-o-shanter. He does not look savage in the least and has rather an intelligent face but of course I had just a passing glance and then went on to Mr. Bain's house ...

When he went on to the mission, McE found Bain to be ill in bed—had not been out of it for a week ... Yesterday he told me he had retched and vomited all week - *McE had to sit up with him ...* he was not violent but talked a lot of nonsense ... this house is situated in a lovely little spot but the whole state of matters is otherwise very disappointing. There is one proper house constructed by Mr. Stewart and Munro in which Mr. Bain lives. There are no partitions, and while his bed is one corner, road goods are piled in another, Coy goods and LMS goods along the side opposite the door, tins of *ufa*, beans and odds and ends scattered about ... The disappointment consists in finding such a state of matters in what is called a mission. The house is nothing but a store very few of its contents belong to the FC and in the disorder which naturally follows Mr. Bain seems to have lost any encouragement to try and have home comforts such are quite possible with a little effort and I find him roughing it with a table and a chair belonging to the road, a chair and bedstead of his own and all the things he possesses for making 'a home' still unpacked.

Of course Mr. Bain is somewhat to blame for all of this as a little firmness would turn out all the offending goods and let the owners take them away ... a little exertion would erect partitions and make the house more habitable and suited to the rainy season but at the same time the FC folks should see that their men are properly supplied with materials for their life and work. The plan which Capt. Hore is endeavouring to have adopted for the Tanganyika Mission of having an industrial department to build houses and carry the supplies for the missionaries is very good. Mr. Bain has been out of calico, flour and many other European necessaries for some time, being quite unable to get them from the Coy, and he has been living on *ufa* and other native productions for some time and I daresay this has something to do with his illness.

August 23

McE describes having only a few hours sleep attending to B who that morning had violent vomiting which lasted till about 1 (i.e. from 9am.) ... I applied turpentine fomentations to the stomach, gave him 18 drops of laudanum in water, and brandy largely diluted with water at frequent intervals but his stomach would retain nothing and the severe retching gradually exhausted itself. Mr. B said the turpentine cloths were the best thing. About two o'clock he was very weak showing symptoms of dysentery and I continued to give him brandy about every hour. He was very feverish but would not allow me to give him quinine at his cooler moments. For some time he wandered a good deal but was lying quiet and about half past three the sickness passed away and left him very sore in his inside. *McE continues to nurse Bain whom he had almost given up, and likewise most of the following day. He goes on to describe various treatments, thinking at one time that B was going to die, but he recovered after several days of vomiting and sickness.*

The chief Maliwanda fearful of an impending attack from the Auremba, comes in asking for powder 'which I refused now as ever' [70]

August 28

McE returning from Maliwanda to Karonga ... At 10.35 I met Mr. Monteith on his way up to the Mwini Wanda en route to Tanganyika with LMS steamer.

August 30

... we were not well on the road before I had to collapse entirely with sickness and vomiting and be carried in a *machila*

August 31 Sunday Karonga

Rather a business Sunday. Quiet feeling of any kind is not encouraged by having 40 blacks jabbering near at hand and too hot a sun to think of taking refuge in another place ... I spent part of the day making an examination of Mr. Stewart's notebook and road accounts concerning the road which have been left here in a box but not gain very much information.

Sept 1

McE sick again and got very little sleep.

Sept 2

After sickness the previous day and still feeling shaky ... after work was over Munro, Nicol and I had a long chat and readings from Burns, etc., etc. as it was to be our last night with him for some time.

---

[70] The official policy of both the mission and the ALC was not to provide gunpowder or arms to Africans or Arabs, but the ALC did not always abide by this – some of their artisans took to gun-running as a profitable sideline.

Sept 3

En route from Karonga to Maramuras. The men all took their loads very willingly tho' some of the boxes were nearer 60 than 50 lbs ... reaching the Rukuru River our men took to the water at once and rolled and splashed and washed evidently to their comfort and enjoyment It was rather a picturesque sight and couples here and there would go into partnership in the washing line and one would sit behind the other—in about 8 ins of water and scrub his neighbour's back well ... Mr. Stewart's road after crossing the Rukuru River takes a roundabout route and has become very overgrown as the natives seldom use it ... saying good-bye to the plain once and for all entered on the Rukuru Valley where the most difficult part of the road construction has been accomplished ... My tent, thanks to Jeannie and Duncan is the acme of perfection. The fly keeps it delightfully cool and the pretty side bags which Mary, Mother, and Jeannie made, look homely and are very useful. I have tried to supplement their efforts by having a nice native mat and the *tout ensemble* is very good and I wish for no better home in Africa in the dry season.

September 4 to 31 December 1884: 'When we return, if return we do'

McEwan makes a start to road work and ends the year at Chirenji

Sept 4
Work started at Maramuras—at last I am able to sit down after a regular day's work on the construction of the road. After due deliberation we decided to begin work here by cleaning a part of the road that has suffered a great deal from land slips the excavation being in steep sidelong ground and the strata lying at a steep downward angle and thus inclining to slip off when left free ... cheered by the way men set to work and other locals joined them—staggered at the rate of progress—about 500 yards in one day. Munro's earlier training of the squad obviously worked ... these men were only black and naked but otherwise they were the very counterpart of 'Hodge' returning from his day's work in the fields only they drink their beer round their fires instead of in the public house.

Sept 6
Munro returned having succeeded in bringing down a large buffalo. Dinner left one too tired to do more than write this journal and snooze over some aneroid calculations.

Sept 7 Sunday
... In the evening we had a visit from Selim who is moving slowly up to his own place. He was with Cameron on his great journey and is well acquainted with the geography of the country west of Tanganyika and we had a talk on these matters, [71] Munro acting as interpreter ... the men went out last night and brought in the buffalo ... all day the place has been reeking with the stench of the meat. The head was enormous ... the horns were certainly a magnificent size but not approaching in grace and beauty those of our own highland cattle.

Sept 8
... dispensed with the swim as a crocodile had been seen in an adjacent pool.

Sept 9
When down for breakfast I was surprised to hear the beat of a drum in the distance and coming out of my tent I saw a small caravan wending its way above this. At the head was a fine stalwart white man—the very representation of Californian Gold Diggers which we see in pictures. Soft white wide-awake slouched over the eyes, grey woollen shirt, waist scarf, white drill trousers, leggings and lacing boots the worse for wear. It was the

---

[71]   Verney Lovett Cameron, another navyman, had made the first ever east-west crossing of Africa in 1873-4 in the course of leading the Livingstone Relief Expedition.

caravan of Lieut. Giraud of the French Navy. He passed Maliwanda on his way westwards more than a year ago with a large and well-equipped caravan, intending to explore the Bangweolo region and go on to the West coast. In this he has not succeeded owing to a constant succession of misfortunes and desertions such as seldom fall to the lot of African travellers. He was travelling at his own expense with a mission from the French Government to explore the Bangweolo district. He looks in splendid health after his harassing experiences and beyond a little dysentery has had no illness to speak of. *McE refers to Victor Giraud finding too late the errors which Ravenstein ascertained from looking again at the original maps, in the maps accompanying Livingstone's Last Journals* - the 'lake' was found to be only reeds and marsh and he lost much equipment due to hostile natives when he had to flee the district. Many of his men deserted hearing of rumours of war between **Stanley** and the Arabs at Tanganyika.

Sept 10
Giraud brings word of Stanley fighting the Arabs in Nanyeuma - and of some influential Arab on Tanganyika having orders to seize anyone selling ivory to the English.[72] *McE reports desertion of the Sokini - one of the tribes working on the road, but they turned up next day.*

Sept 12
Near the Lufira river McE reports a very fertile area supporting potatoes, tamarinds, bananas, castor oil plant, etc, etc. and refers to writing to Oban again.

Sept 14
... When going through Mwiniwanda's village green, a *mwavi* drinking was going on and I may be lucky in seeing one as the natives are not particularly anxious about this supreme rite of theirs being seen. However Maliwanda was quite affable and endeavoured to explain to me the cause of the present ceremony. A man with his wife and two children had come from Minipoko to live with him and to make sure all was right he has to drink *mwavi*. Mwini Wanda said the man offered to drink the stuff so he made it weak and consequently he vomited and was all right. *Mwavi* spelt 'Muave' by Dr. Laws but *muravi* would be better ... to drink m*wavi* is the African's god and is better than arbitration. They are too great liars for a judicial council to be of much use, but the joke of *mwavi* is that suppose Mwini Wanda accuses a chief of some crime against him that chief will immediately offer to drink *mwavi* to prove he is innocent and it is Mwini Wanda who makes up the poison for him to drink and the old boy has sometimes told

---

[72] There was fierce competition for ivory between the Arabs and the ALC, who hoped to displace the Arabs from this lucrative trade – it was only the sale of ivory which kept the ALC solvent, since none of the other agricultural products were profitable without an available local market.

Bain that he knew so-and-so was guilty and meant to make the mixture strong and vice versa. When a big *mwavi* bout is on the surrounding chiefs turn out in force.[73]

Sept 15
McE reports that his collapses are taking place regularly once a fortnight.

Sept 20th
Argues with Bain over necessity of taking chronometer rates—doesn't improve his opinion of Bain.

Sept 21
... too ill today to take any observations. The fever and sickness were both very troublesome excepting for a little while in the afternoon when Bain read me a sermon by Bushnell. Bain has theories about the mail arriving tonight but we looked for it in vain. I wish it would come.

Sept 22
For want of the mail I took two old letters and read most of the home ones so that I am quite prepared for the later news. I received my last mail at Maruru on 25 June so that after all I have only been without letters for three months which I suppose is not very unreasonable for this country.

Sept 26
... it is a most enjoyable (*referring to daily bath*) and refreshing daily event even in a stagnant pool - we get the boys to throw basins of water over us which makes a very good shower bath. While we were bathing the vanguard of an Arab caravan came over the hill and soon a goodly number was gathered under the shade of the trees ... We found on enquiry that the Arab was Mlozi who has a village near Karambos on the Rukuru.[74] While we were at dinner he and his immediate followers appeared and the chief men sat around at the door of the tent and we had a long chat about things in general. I am rather a silent member of those scenes as I do not know the language and Munro does most of the talking. He knew Mlozi of old having repaired his musical boxes and showed him kindness at different times. Mlozi looks more of the gentleman than Selim—the first Arab I encountered. He does not give one the same impression of crafty cunning as that man and seems a nicer man altogether. (Mlozi was returning from the south with ivory) His retinue and carriers form quite an addition to our little colony. They have camped here for the night and now the whole place is studded with their *nsasa* or light bivouacs

---

[73]   The missionaries attempted to stop the tradition of *mwavi* drinking as a method of settling disputes without success.

[74]   Despite McEwan's favourable impression, Mlozi was in fact a notorious slave trader who later fought the Europeans in the so-called Arab wars. He was gracious to whites when it suited his purposes, but was both cunning and ruthless.

made of branches, etc. The Arabs take with them their harem. I believe Mlozi has five or six young girls as his wives, but they are kept well concealed as a rule.[75]

On such a night as this one cannot complain of African life being dull, lonely, or uninteresting. We are camped in a little hollow down which the native path to the stream some seventy yards distant. Mr. Munro's tent and my own are pitched close together. On one side there is a large *nsasa*[76] in which the Atonga sleep but at present they are a little lively after their evening meal and while one group imitates the dances of their mortal enemy - the Angonis - another lot are discussing some stirring topic. I suppose *nsuma* might be considered a stirring topic. On the other side of the path the Sokinis have their quarters, working harder through the day they are more silent at night than their noisy neighbours opposite.

On the higher ground there are little groups of Arab followers squatting round their fires and making themselves comfortable for the night. Between the moon and the great roaring fires of our workers, the scene is well illuminated and one sees many picturesque scenes—perhaps a well-made handsome Arab boy carrying a gourd of water to his master, perhaps a few plainer men lugging along a large tusk to make it snug and safe. The costumes are various in size and quality ranging from the piece of string and square foot of calico that serves the Sokini to the more elaborate and pretty costume of the Arab's long spotless white overshirt—handsome waist scarf and heavy turban or in the cool of the day, little white skull cap. Some of the intermediate rigs are no less interesting. I saw one little fellow with the mane of a zebra round his brow making the top of his like a huge starfish. Mlozi and his factotum paid us a visit at night and we sat talking till nearly eleven. His man, hearing that we wanted some rice sent off at once and brought me a canful and when I gave him a candle he was indignant at my appearing to buy food, that being a great breach of Arab etiquette. Mlozi, quite unsolicited promised that when he got to his village his women would pound a lot of rice and send it to me.

Oct 1

There is no word of the mail and we languish accordingly but endeavour to possess our souls in patience.

Oct 3

… the long looked for mail arrived, but owing to the complications on the Shire no home letters had come. We received news of Capt. Foote's death and truly we seem to be in better circumstances than people further south.[77]

---

[75]   It is interesting that Munro in his diary for this day makes much more of the necessity for a road re-alignment than this vivid description of the Arab camp by McEwan.
[76]   *Nsasa* is a temporary shelter made of local materials.
[77]   This refers to serious native disturbances on the Shire with attacks on the ALC stations and the sinking of the *Lady Nyassa*, sister vessel of the *Ilala*, plying on the Shire, described by Munro.

Oct 5

McE has rather maudlin observations on a sermon by Robertson relating to the dear departed and the closeness of family - obviously echoing McE's thoughts at this time. McE then says ... after tea I tried to impart some of my admiration of Ruskin to Munro by reading a few paragraphs of *The Mystery of Life*, etc.

Oct 7

... on opening ammonia bottle the concern burst in my face—I washed out with fingers in eye—kicked over table with all my chemicals, howled for Munro. Luckily the ammonia tho' strong did not do more than nip and I was soon able to investigate matters and found all my developing chemicals smashed and scattered so I will have to give up that part of my work. I tremble for the rest of my plates and hope they may keep to be developed at home.

Oct 9

McE reports completing a mile in 4 days but much troubled by toothache—at night in desperation tried large doses of laudanum, carbolic acid, water and brandy, chlorodyn—lay in pain all night.

Oct 11

Attempt at extraction futile (a three-pronger)

Oct 14

McE reports on a dispute between two men, one punching the other on the nose resulting in profuse bleeding, the older man with the bleeding nose accusing the other of still being a child because he still slept with his mother ... etc, etc.

Oct 15

Remarkable 860 yards done albeit on easy ground, McE laying out all day.

Oct 18

McE reports a week's run of 1 mile 130 yards ... which cheers us mightily—Munro shot two zebra—when M came in there was a great skirling of small birds going on in a tree close at hand so took the gun and shot one and devoted the evening to skinning it guided by these invaluable *Hints*.[78] It is slightly bigger than our sparrow with yellow and black feathers and red or scarlet eyes. Wrote journal and bed at 9.30 happy and content, pretty well longing for the mail, looking forward to Sunday's rest and wondering how all goes on at home.

Oct 20

Mr. Monteith arrived in camp at 5.30 pm on his way from Maliwanda to the lake. He has made a very speedy journey to Lake Tanganyika and back. After tea had a long chat

---

[78] The *Hints* referred to were the periodic publications by the Royal Geographical Society under the title *Hints for Travellers* – with advice on everything from first aid to stuffing birds.

about road prospects. His opinion condensed is that the road should be made in 3 years. that it is very desirable to have it if the Coy was a Coy but in the meantime it is not. He returns disgusted with everything and everybody but himself and in a mood that does not help to make life pleasant either to self or companion. (n.b. *Munro makes a similar comment*)

Oct 28

In the evening the men came to ask (?) home seeing the rains had come but they were well pleased with our definite decision that they should all return in the steamer when next she went south in about 5 weeks. We then explained our Tanganyika journey and asked for carriers - names to be given in tomorrow night.[79] This is quite a lively road—we have had two or three lots of caravans today, including Fitima going home. After rain the air is beautifully clear and delightfully cool and we see hills we have not seen before. One we take to be Mount Waller but are not sure.

Better still today 1640 yds. I have not been able to fix the latitude of this place owing to a completely clouded sky.

Oct 31

... while busy a messenger arrived from Karonga with a note saying steamer was in sight and mails would be sent off at once. This set us in "a palpitation orful". At 11 o'clock work was stopped and the loads taken on 2 miles to the Lufira R. where we pitched what is likely to be our last camp of this season's work as the two miles are difficult work and heavy. We are glad to get near a running stream so as to have good water and our daily bathe. We arranged everything well, gave the men half a holiday to build *nsasas* for themselves and had got comfortably settled when the boys came in with the long looked for and much welcome mail. First fevers and first mails are equally interesting episodes in African life but of course for pleasure the latter has it.

I was very much relieved and very pleased to have such good news from home but a little disappointed at not having letters from Largs.[80] The news is interesting—engagements, marriages, trips, summer holidays, notes about old friends. valuable cooking recipes from Jeannie. Graphics, Illustrated London News, Pall Mall Budget, Weekly Times, and Punches *ad libitum* and also Geographical Proceedings which I value most. Bain and Smith arrived in camp about 7.30 en route from Maliwanda to the steamer so we had them in camp for the night. The mail brings word of Elmslie's appointment to Angone and the steamer brings an LMS missionary for Tanganyika - Mr. Harris.

---

[79] This would be the continuation north westwards towards the south end of lake Tanganyika along the proposed line of the Stevenson Road.

[80] It is assumed that this is a reference to James Stevenson who lived in Largs, in Scotland.

Nov 2

Copying Mr. Stewart's paper on "The Glacial Period of Lake Nyasa' and reading most of the day. *McE records among others, writing to Mr. Stevenson to whom he appears to have a direct line.*

Nov 5

I couldn't help remembering just now that exactly a year ago I was driving in a hansom from the Westminster Palace Hotel to 8 King's Road bonfires blazing in most directions and never a thought crossing my mind of being in Central Africa with a year or two of them. However all matters seem to go smoothly and I am happy unless my coming away has made others unhappy. Anxious, it certainly has, but I do not think unhappy, at least I am not told so. In reading over the newspapers which came by the last mail (my first mail) ... I would rather know that those whom I love are unhappy and suffering, even tho' I could not help.

... Harris left for Maliwanda this morning. He gave us much news but talks in such a fashion of his journey and of other people that I fear he will get little sympathy in case of accident or failure. Everybody in this country talks too much about the other people. Not a person I have met but is tarred with the dreadful sinful stick and I at least try to have done with it. Out here it seems so unchristian and so unright and I am sure leads to much unpleasantness, cold shoulders and bad feeling which in many cases has very poor reasons.

Nov 14

McEwan comments on the men's delight in finishing the season's work, stating that they had done 17 miles on the road, then goes on to Karonga.

Nov 22-Dec 7

Preparing for journey to Tanganyika - steamer long overdue, but they will wait a week before starting. Munro and McE in very good health ... but hanging on is a deadly process in Africa.

Dec 8

McE says no steamer in sight ... actually rummaged out my fiddle and rigged it up for action and strummed a few tunes in the evening. Munro and Monteith stood it pretty well and actually asked for more, which they got.

Dec 10

Steamer comes saw that Morrison and not Harkness was doing engineer duty—I had letters of 1 October from Mary and James and of 29 October from Jeannie ... I did my best to send long letters to make up for long silence and wrote 11 letters, mother,

Jeannie, Jennie and John, Reid, Mrs. McD, Thom Moffat, 2 to Stevenson, Mrs. Fort, O'Neill, Kirk, and a local mail to Dr. Scott, Hetherwick, Moir, Elmslie, Bain, Smith.[81]

Dec 14

Spent a quiet restful Sunday reading a little and thinking more—earnestly hoping for a successful journey and wondering what news will be waiting for us when we return, if return we do. I take ship's chronometer which I rate as well as the weather would admit- mer. barometer - 2 aneroids - 6" sextant - 10" sextant stand and horizontal prismatic compass - max and min thermometer - Abney level, chain, watch and beyond Raper, the NA and other books necessary for notes and calculations. I have only Ruskin's 2 vols, Robertson 1 vol and the revised version.(*of the Bible.*)

Dec 15

This was our starting day ... Our men seem well pleased with their loads, tho' some seem heavy enough but they all diminish as time goes as they are mostly provisions and cloth without which no one travels here. We get good chances to study black character among our men. On the whole it is rather black especially as regards truthfulness, gratitude and honesty. We have been rather down at the chiefs, Kasingula, Karambo for not giving us men. They delight to see one in a fix and take every advantage of it by asking pay, presents. etc[82] ... We are now in the plain near Karambo's village and at the entrance to the Rukuru Valley. When one looks at the hills near the edge of the plain, Mr. Stewart's glacier theory seems very plausible as the line of the hills edging the plain seems just to have been burst through in two places the continuation of the existing hills forming a very evident connection across the openings ... got a magnificent view of the Nyanja and the Livingstone Mountains.

Dec 16

McE reports trouble with men and attempted to get resolution.

Dec 17

... Mivi Charanga has taken up quarters here and is busy building houses. He is a victim of the Angone and was driven out of his last village. His defences are unique. We were going down to the river to wash when he came running after us and going in front proceeded to pull up about 20 wooden spikes and a few yards ahead another 20 or so and then to remove thorny bushes ... rather astonished the natives by appearing in a pair of light ? sleeping trousers with an immense patch of fiery red flannel on the back. They thought it was very good but the camp joke was the attempts of the men to lift a drop of mercury. One by one they would come forward boldly scorning the inability of their unsuccessful brethren and then when they failed they would take to their heels quite

---

[81]   The reference to Kirk is most likely Sir John Kirk, the remarkable British Consul in Zanzibar, who had been on Livingstone's first journey up the Zambezi, and who liked to keep his finger on the pulse of anything that was happening in East and Central Africa.

[82]   This coincides with Munro's views.

ashamed of themselves and amid the convulsions of all the men. They quite roared especially when the chief himself took to his heels.

Dec 18

Mr. M got to the village well ahead of me and when I arrived he was sitting in glorious ease on a native mat with a pot of native beer before him. These pots are rather baskets made of closely woven reeds and are quite watertight - I think the Chinyanja name is *dukiva*. The chief's wife had done the honours in the absence of her lord and master. She is rather a good looking woman which I suppose induced M to give her a whole yard of cloth for the beer and she in her gratitude at receiving so much more than its value soon appeared at our tent with another lot of beer ... neither of us was so far gone as to be able for a drink of beer so we went in for a regular brewing.[83] The *morraa* as the natives prepare it consists of the grain and water in a consistency something like mud. They usually mix this with some hot water and drink the whole but not particularly anxious to burden our stomachs to that extent we first poured the original concoction into a handkerchief and then pouring hot water on to it allowed the whole to strain through and got a splendid drink. Then we left the machinery outside and left it to strain till morning. Mr. Munro enlivened the evening a little by trying to catch moths in the tent with an enormous butterfly net.[84]

Dec 19

... found Bain's house in a deplorable mess as also the garden and grounds. The mud plaster was off the walls in many places leaving nothing but the strips of palms and admitting just a little more weather than is good at this season of the year ... The ground behind was a garden of weeds and the house itself was filthy. Of course M 'walled over' Pemba the man in charge, but he said the master wanted to have the house that way, meaning with the mud off for the sake of ventilation!

... I cannot but be sorry for this so-called 'mission' more especially as Bain is now at Bandawe merely to spend Christmas and writes ' I am not quite sure in my own mind that I do right to remain.' I have no doubt that he does very wrong. He ought to be here getting his house and ground ready for the rainy season which has now set in. I hope in writing this I may not be accused of presumption especially as I myself am just on the eve of failing in my Tanganyika expedition or at any rate may require to curtail it to a great extent. As I recorded before our men on the way up complained a great deal about their loads and threatened to run away so that it best to be plain with them so shortly after arriving we called a *mirandu* and told them that those who meant to run away to run now as we propose to get more men ...

---

[83] Given Munro's reputation for abstemiousness, it is perhaps not surprising that his description of this incident is somewhat different.

[84] Munro's collection of some 70 different butterfly species still survives in remarkably good condition in its original glass case.

Dec 21

... two of our men got into a row with the natives over a beer drinking and we had a long noisy *mirandu* over that. I would rather flog our men even if they deserted and spoiled our journey than see the natives here taken advantage of. It would inevitably affect the credit of the white man and so the mission - the black people here cannot as yet distinguish between the coy, mission and road. I read a little of *Romola* and liked it well. When I remember the enjoyment I derived from *Adam Bede* and the pleasant and profitable reading which *Romola* promises, I think to Ruskin and Robertson I must add George Eliot as the components of a small travelling library.

Dec 22

McE again refers to scarcity of men which will curtail journey to Tanganyika.

Dec 23

McE describes early packing with reduced loads hoping for more men - refers to following route of Stewart and Ross. The road has been constructed by digging two parallel ditches about 10 or 12 feet apart and throwing the excavation into the centre thus forming a raised roadway about 8 or 9 feet in width. This mode of construction even if it was suitable and successful was too elaborate and occupies too much time in proportion to present requirements on this route. Almost throughout the entire length we traversed today the edges of the formation have been gradually washed away, narrowing the available road so that it forms only a good footpath falling away on each side. I am more convinced than ever that nothing should be done but such work as comes under the term 'clearing'. Taking out obstructive trees to a width of 7 or 8 ft and making no attempt at a formation except in sidelong ground where of course there is no alternative.[85]

... near villages the older people in this region are now quite accustomed to the sight of the white man but the children usually scatter in all directions, the younger ones rushing to the maternal bosom or often the maternal back and nesting there, and ostrich-like burying their faces away from the dread spectacle of the man in clothes. When I opened the tripod of my compass near Fitimas there was a movement of alarm among the herd boys which developed into a wholesale flight when my eye went to the prism ... I shall be curious to know if the chief intends to extend his stockade or feels a confidence from being adjacent to the white man's road. I should like to believe the latter but in the meantime cannot. We noticed today at the side of the road a native smelting furnace.

On arrival at a native forge was in full swing one man was reforging a hoe, another a spear. The apparatus consists of a hollow in the ground where *macalla* (charcoal) is put and lighted—the leader from the bellows is a conical earthenware pipe about 8 inches long—the narrower end is in the centre of the furnace while the large mouth is filled with a hollow tube of bamboo which comes from the bellows - these last consist of some animal skin worked till it is very pliable and formed into the shape of a bag, a hole being made where the bamboo is inserted. *McE then goes on to describe operation of forge ...*

---

[85]   Despite the road being marked on maps for many years afterwards as if it was a main thoroughfare, it remained largely a cleared footpath, unsuitable for vehicular traffic.

The inhabitants of Furza's (?) are more decently clad than other Konde or Wana people—they are also more open—not quite so impudent and seem quite industrious. Another industry we saw going on was making bark cloth ... The huts are very well constructed - I had a high old time sketching in the afternoon. I have not yet come across a people so little afraid of books and pencils. They submitted to being sketched quite willingly and even accommodated me by remaining in one position ... M had a good sweat after we carried him to bed - holus bolus into the tent. Took a big tea at 7 and is now all right. My turn next.

Dec 24
Describes forge going well with double bellows - *everything seems the same as what Livingstone met with between Nyasa and Bangweolo, says McE. Munro was worse and they determined to return in the morning. Munro was often in these bouts also affected by jaundice.*

Dec 25
... who could think of Christmas with the surroundings of an African village ... M was looking bad this morning. I myself wasn't feeling quite the thing, but it doesn't do for two white men to be ill at once, so of course I gave way ...

Dec 26 (Cherenji)
Both unwell and remained in bed ... difficult to get fowls for food except at extortionate prices.

Dec 28
I cannot realise that this is the last Sabbath of the year tho' I did think a good deal about '85 and its prospects ... came across some sermons by Beecher which was most enjoyable. Munro worse fainting and with some symptoms of jaundice reappearing. I had no wish to nurse anything in Africa other than fever and had no hesitation in arranging that he should go to Bandawe while still strong enough to be moved ... Write to Mother, Jeannie, Mr. Stevenson, and Dr. Scott.

Dec 29 (Cherenji)
Starts to improve the house ... I have divided the house so that one half goes to the occupier and the other half as a store. There will be comfortable room for three beds and another could get a place in an emergency. If it should ever happen that ladies grace this place with their presence even for one night—the little room can easily be curtained off.

Dec 31 (Cherenji)
... Perhaps it is rather a liberty putting Bain's possessions into something like decent order but nothing is so easy as to put them back in their old style and indeed I am not at all certain that they won't get back to that very soon unless the last trip to Bandawe has had a new effect. Half expected a mail today but it was after all unreasonable to think it would arrive under a 'half-expectation' when weeks of 'whole expectation' don't sometimes fetch it. Out of sheer desperation I took up a short life of Hegel the German

philosopher and found it not so unpalatable as I expected ... after getting into bed the rain came down in great deluges as if bent on washing out all the evil of 1884, the good can stand a shower or two. Of course I was in Crieff tonight, remembering '83 and imagining '84 and '85. [86]

The next 4 pages of the diary are dedicated to a Daily Record for 1885 from 1st January including date, place, thermometer and barometer readings, rainfall, general remarks on weather, health, medicine taken, and special occurrences. The medicines taken regularly include quinine, Eno's salts, chlorodyne, opium, rhubarb pills, magnesia, saline. This record ends on May 8 with Munro down with jaundice.

---

[86]   There is no indication of what the association with Crieff in Scotland was – it might have been family celebrations there at Hogmanay.

January 1 to May 8 1885: 'How thankful I am for all that has happened'

McEwan ill with fever at Mwiniwanda, returns to Bandawe, before returning to recommence work on road.

Jan 1 1885
Ill with fever.

Jan 2
In these fevers I think it was foolish to leave such a healthy place as old Scotland—will never come to Africa again and so on in that strain, but in health no thoughts of that kind come to the fore and I long only for the rainy season to be over so that we may get to work on the road. *(McE was not better for at least 10 days, while Munro was recuperating at Bandawe until 23 February.)*

Jan 11
I was very bad with violent purging early in the morning took quinine which little effect—read a short sermon by Robertson before breakfast and devoted most of the day to a home letter—my first this year. While at breakfast Mwini Wanda came up with a number of his followers to tell Mr. Bain that he was going to drink *Mwavi* at Nyambera's the chief who massacred Mr. Stewart's men the first year of the road work. Mwini Wanda had bought a cow from Nyambera who said it would calve. Wanda says it won't calve and is a very bad cow. N asserts that it is quite good so M.W. offers to drink the *Mwavi* to prove his case. This is the great intertribal and inter-individual arbitration and a most evil and superstitious one it is. The drink will be prepared by Nyambera and if M.W. vomits it he will have won his case, otherwise he dies. He thus displays great incredulity and great trust in one and the same person and I suppose he's quite aware that N is very probably afraid to poison him. Mr. B tries to persuade him of the dire absurdity of the whole proceeding, but M.W. will not give up such an old established and universal custom. In the afternoon, I had a short spell on Mr. B's portable harmonium, after tea read a little from a book by Fleming Stevenson called *Praying and Working* and got to bed at half past eight.

January 12
This evening I have been writing up my recent barometer observations for altitudes but the various books I have are all so conflicting in regard to the expansion of mercury per degree Far.

January 13
Bain was bad with fever ... I was busy all day with the men, erecting a railing, digging out and making new drains. Took hourly observations of the barometer today. Started

today to write up my experiences of outfit etc. either for the use of other people or to aid me should I have occasion to put out for Africa again.

January 14

... at dinner time we heard a shot and Mr. Monteith soon appeared. He has come up to get LMS steamer forwarded but does not at present intend to go himself.

January 15

... In the afternoon Mwiniwanda returned from his *mwavi* drinking. He had some goats with him and had evidently come off with flying colours.

January 18

The usual quiet Sunday ... we had a discussion last night as to what position we would and should assume in the case of one of our employees offending against local natives. We assumed a case in which one of our boys had committed a very serious offence against a native, the punishment of which according to native law would be getting a foot cut off. Mr. B. maintained that he would hand his man over to the local chief to be dealt with according to native law having first assured himself of the truth of the accusation. On pressing he admitted he would expostulate with the chief on the punishment but not having effect he would allow him to take his boy and deal with him. In stating this he made no exceptions regarding punishments however barbarous. He declines to be chief of his men even when they are imported natives from Bandawe or elsewhere and he says they will only have his protection while they behave.

For a missionary of all people I think the position is most unChristian and indefensible. However were the contretemps to arise and I were present I would at once take the man into my employ and act as his chief rather than have him committed to the tender mercies of untutored savages. Mr. B. acting as he would, would only be perpetuating and countenancing barbarism. When in Africa the men in my employ will be my tribe and I shall be their chief—they will neither be tried, condemned or punished by any law of native ideas but by my own ideas of justice, or if there are more white men there, *our* ideas. The result of any other policy must be ruinous as it will place the mission of the white man in a very untruthful light. *McEwan then goes on to quote from one of Ward Beecher's sermons on the point to support his view.*

Jan 19

Mr. B and I went prospecting across the stream to see if we could gather information as to what would be the best site for a permanent station. *McE provides sketch to show alternative positions with detail of logistics such as transport of water, etc.*

Jan 20

McE had mirandu with men regarding future work on the road and to clarify conditions etc ... of course they all have an intention of returning in two months - but they are black men - and that means "don't believe them till you see them". The nasty pain is here again and I must lie down to get a little ease. *McE describes a dance in the local village* ... The younger villagers were standing in a circle, one side being the young boys and men—the other sex taking the other side. The only instrumental music was two young men playing drums and the others sang a kind of chant accompanied with clapping of the hands. The dance had only a little method in it—the men would jump into the circle playing antics and making grimaces then catch girls by the waist and then they danced a *pas de deux* the girls meanwhile looking most meek and casting their eyes down to the ground. Never more than two girls danced at a time—when one was tired, another taking her place.

The women did not sing at all for which we were sorry ... I am anxious to get boy from Fitima's and such a fine cheery set of boys to select from I have not seen in Africa. To teach them I imagine would be a great pleasure. I cannot help thinking that some strong-minded and noble man who would go *among* these people (not beside them) - and establish and maintain a very evident superiority by teaching them industrial arts and the younger ones their letters and besides both a practical and not a doctrinal or theological Christianity would do immeasurable good.

Jan 21
... in the afternoon a great squad of men came from Wiwa to carry LMS steamer and before dark, Mr. M's men returned from the lake with calico so he will be in his glory tomorrow. At present, he is a man with one idea and he will persist in dinning us with speculations as to where his *olendos* are etc, etc. etc.[87] Read with great delight Goshen's speech on the second reading of the Franchise Bill. His peroration was noble and more noble for its want of dogmatism.

Jan 22
... Mr. B seems to think like me that it is as well when on a special errand to a native to introduce it as such and not slip it in underhand so after the usual salutations, Mr. B told him what I wanted. Fitima then turned to the boys that were hanging around and asked which would go but they all hung back. One impudent little fellow whom I had noticed making grimaces when down last time volunteered and rolled his eyes ... so he was out of the running at once. I said a boy called Chiruvia was the one I wanted but he was a modest little fellow, hung his head, and bolted on the first opportunity. Rather than risk not getting him we said I would come down in three days and take the boy he would give - two if he liked.

January 24
After a contretemps with the local chief, McE says ... This experience only adds to my present conviction that a very hard and fast line must be drawn between the mission and the company in any future arrangements and let that line be drawn as soon as possible. It is very evident that the natives cannot perhaps will not distinguish between the co, mission and road. The sins or supposed offences of all will be visited on the others and the only step that will lead to the distinction being made is a total separation of their

---

[87]   *Ulendo* (correct spelling) can be a file of men, caravan, or more strictly a journey as in *safari* (Kiswahili).

stations and of their work. At present the mission completely loses any individuality it may possess owing to it being made the home of the co's agents when they come here.

In the meantime such hospitality could not be courteously refused but as soon as possible an understanding should be arrived at which will prevent the co from utilising mission premises or very adjacent ground for the purpose of storing goods in transit for forming a station with which its accompaniments of howling carriers, angry disputes over payment, buying of ivory, etc would in great measure nullify what is considered as missionary work.[88]

McE instances Monteith's activities in receiving and dispatching goods making quiet study impossible—McE refers to reading the same paragraph of a book many times over. Complains about Monteith without asking permission occupying the house entrance to conduct negotiations for buying ivory—according to McE, Monteith is not a man of many ideas - claims that they have had to put up with him hour after hour with repeated speculation of where olendos will be or and when so and so will return—how many men are gone—how many loads remain and while we are very well pleased when olendos are successful we, at least I, cannot stand a constant dinning and repetition of useless remarks, more painful even in their mindless monotony.

Jan 25

Even in Africa, Sundays always seem a brighter and better day than others ... I spent the forenoon with Robertson and Ruskin ... *referring to his preference for restrained writing rather than oratory, McE says* I feel how much better, if I ever should have to record my experience of Africa, it will be to refrain from the superficial accounts of travel given in popular books which are so successful and write for the information not for the amusement of the reader. All scientific men from Huxley downwards condemn very strongly the want of scientific method and exactness in the descriptions of such authors.

Jan 31

... have been thinking somewhat how we are to do the best towards developing the country and in my mind at least these thoughts are very much quickened by an intense dissatisfaction with the business arrangements and aims of the ALC. I shouldn't be surprised some day to hear myself designating it with sincere conviction 'perhaps unintentionally but not the less surely a disorganised hypocrisy'.[89]

Feb 1

McE reads Robertson again, saying he never thought a man with such Christian conviction could be so miserable. Conjectures about the wisdom of preaching heaven to the natives as simply a place where they will have a better life than on earth and what is

---

[88] McEwan obviously felt very strongly about this issue i.e. the confusion in the native mind between the mission, the ALC and its commercial activities, and the road building, where their respective representatives were in close proximity.

[89] The ALC was unique among trading companies in Africa in having both commercial objectives and ostensibly a Christian ethos, which resulted in neither being fulfilled satisfactorily.

the best way of presenting Christianity ... so far I only work by being interested in them, loving them, and being kind to them and dealing them a strict justice and however much the work of the mission and the missionaries has my wishes for success I do not feel that I am ever likely to work otherwise.

Feb 2
Makes detailed sketch and notes on the outlet of the Rukuru river into Lake Nyasa with compass bearings and soundings—obviously with a view to considering a harbour here. Also shot about 40 wildfowl.

February 3
... Some of Mr. Stewart's notes which I was reading today referred to the flogging cases at Blantyre and Livingstonia and here is a passage in one of F W Robertson's letters which I also came across today "I am still, *in many cases* for the Christian virtue of an English oak with an English hand to lay it on, and show mercy when you have done justice".[90]

Feb 5
Referring to steamer delays and disappointments McE says ... It is scandalous even in Central Africa that there should be so little business system. On no grounds whatsoever can it be justified. Probable excuses are numerous. In the first place it is said that there are so many uncontrollable circumstances that it is impossible to run to dates ... it seems so inevitable that I shall have to oppose myself to anyone who supports the company as being what it ought to and might be or near it that I have started a private notebook in reference to this alone. In this 'hanging on' condition of mind it is almost impossible to settle to work of any kind.[91] I just remembered that this was my birthday and forgot again till now. I hope I am wiser than a year ago and may the process continue. I sometimes wonder that I didn't feel more regret during these days of packing in the dining room with Mother and Mary. Will next 5th see us together again I wonder.

Feb 7
... saw a man and his wife industriously engaged in making bark cloth. They had hammer formed of a small rhino horn with a wooden handle so the front being cut diamond shaped. It is not often one sees husband and wife working together. Occasionally the father gets the baby to hold. But still I have never seen women degraded as is often spoken of. They cook the food, clean the hut and have the garden sometimes but it never seems unnatural. Once or twice I have seen the man returning with trees to build his

---

[90]   These cases carried out by the missions caused a furore at home and much adverse press criticism: at this time the missions assumed some responsibility for civil administration within their stations.

[91]   These delays and enforced idleness had a serious effect on the morale of staff and is confirmed by frequent references in Munro's diary.

house but I suppose he was content with having cut them and that it is not unreasonable that his better half should have her share so she was carrying them home.

Feb 11

Mr. M made a calculation today based on Mr. Moir's last letter from which he deduced that the steamer might have gone into dock to be painted and that we might expect her tomorrow. That letter was the most deplorable example of indecision that I ever remember to have seen. It was interspersed with such lines as these Dec, Mar. February (nb first two crossed out). At the top of the page one date was given and contradicted at the bottom without any reference to the previous statement and after two pages of the most remarkable time table abounding with safety clauses the whole effort was practically cancelled and rendered doubtful by a question at the bottom addressed to Mr. Monteith "Can she (the *Ilala*) go so long unpainted, etc. What on earth the agent at a land station was to know regarding a steamer which he had only been on board as agent, never for any purpose other than bringing off mails or seeing about cargo I really don't know—and this is one of the hand that has 'been stretched out to save Africa'! Poor Africa with only such a salvation. When they get to know the ALC they may perhaps pray to be saved from, not by the Coy. Of these remarks, prejudice or unkind, they are all together conceived from a growing experience culminating for the present in that discreditable letter. One businessman at home sending such a letter to another businessman would keep his reputation only till the letter was read. I wish it was sent to Mr. C while I was office boy at 175. Pleasant thoughts of Mary's birthday. May she never get into the clutches of the ALC.

Feb 13

Mail arrives ... brings word of the death of Mrs Moir's baby—I had 29 letters.

Feb 14

... am thankful to get such good news from home. But nothing from S.[92]

Feb 24

McE says travelling boxes depend on what sort of journey, whether observations are to be taken, etc ... whether observations are to be taken or the compass only to be used for mapping. There is no doubt that if a country is to be mapped it involves a great addition to what has to be taken and what has to be done on and after the journey but I am glad that it makes me uncomfortable to go over ground without carefully noting it and taking necessary bearings. I believe that but for this my journeys would equal most people's for speed etc. but at present I am the slow traveller of the district taking three and a half days to what others do in 3 but they don't take time to notice that spiders weave at this season more than at any other and other little items

---

[92] Almost certainly this refers to Stevenson, who appears to have become less interested in his project.

McE then goes on to give very detailed account of the architecture of the villages and huts, the making of pottery, clothing and appearance of the natives, gardens, crops etc.—very good observation near Mweni Wanda's.[93]

Sketch by Donald Munro of Nkonde village houses

McE had recruited a young attendant called Sambo among other boys ... It is very pleasant on the march to have young boys in our company. They are lively, free-spirited and the four of them walked along very briskly laughing and talking very immoderately very much like the manner of home children when out for a day in the country.

Feb 25
... arrived at Mweni Pangal's village—describes chief. About 200 huts much space taken up by native granaries—no cattle because of tsetse.

Feb 26
Detailed description of making of cotton cloth.

February 27
(First anniversary of leaving home.) Just a year tonight since I said my first real good bye to those at home and a harder and more sorrowful business than I imagined was possible. I trust the 'How are you' if we live to see it will be correspondingly pleasant. No one knows how thankful I am for all that has happened during the past 12 months as much at home as here.

When taking aneroid readings at the top of the hill I discovered that my aneroid barometer had been broken on the way up. It must have been done by my boy who carried it a short time at the start, and then I had it put in the barrel of a gun, where they travel very safely. However I must underline a note for next journey 'Therms to be

---

[93] It is symptomatic of their different styles of observation that these detailed descriptions are largely absent from Munro's diary.

carried in metal cases lined with indiarubber tubing'. A trip like today impels my ideas most irresistably towards a three years' science course under Huxley if funds are available. I think 3 years anchorage at home on my return might throw me out of good opportunities for resuming work here but I hope that events will hinder me from coming back to Africa without first acquiring such a science training as will enable me to let others have some value from what is to be seen and known.

March 1

Looking forward to a quiet contemplative Sunday, McE complains about Bain not making it clear to locals that this should be so. (He refers to several rivers one of which is shown on Thomson's map i.e. the Lukua).

March 2

... A lot of Wandaa's men were knocking about today but all of a sudden they grabbed their spears and went off like so many wild hares. They told us the village drum was sounding—the Chimbimbi—as they call it and wherever they may be when it sounds they must all make for the village post haste. It may be war or anything else. Today it was generally supposed to be war with the Wasingwa with whom Wanda has some *mirandu.* We saw today what a helpless position the mission would be in a case of war in this district. Of course the people fear him, not on account of his guns, but merely because he is the white man but they must discover sooner or later that they could demolish the white man and his belongings with perfect ease in a forenoon and when that is realised the guns will be required—far better to have missions well equipped in that line at first. In the evening we asked what the Chimbimbi had been beating for and they said because a leopard had leapt the stockade of the village and had taken away a goat. *McE refers to reading his Bible on the long hard years God gave Joseph among the Egyptians before allowing him to exert his influence—must it not also be right in the case of Foreign Missions.*

March 5

Evils of procrastination—because of morning mist failed to get observations ... at one place a great beer drinking was in operation. About 50 men both old and young were seated in a broken elipse all with native made drinking cup which was being filled with beer by one of the young men to which a small boy added a quantity of hot water—some of the men had their faces barbarously coloured with a brilliant vermillion which they concoct from a local tree. We did not linger long—just remaining for about 5 minutes till our men had partaken of the black brothers' hospitality. Some of the worthies were decidedly 'fu' at what seemed the beginning of the carnival.

... after we had pitched our tent Chinga came out to greet us. Mr. B gave him a present at once of five or six yards. He brought some sour sweet milk, some native beer and some cobs. Mr. B asked to have some sweet milk as we wanted to have porridge. He has peculiar views as to how one should get what they want at a village. I wanted to send my men to get milk to buy but refrained in deference to Mr. B who was boss of the expedition and the consequence was that we went to bed without porridge and milk and in a very bad temper at the failure of the purveyor I had a drink of some native beer with warm water added and turned over to sleep feeling very feverish. Just when getting comfortable Mr. B began to create a disturbance in the tent over his precious keys which he never knows where to find. This time they were clean gone and he arrived at the conclusion that they must have tumbled out of his pocket at the place where we bathed.

March 6

McE describes a native bridge of bamboo roped together with creepers ... The accesses would hardly have been approved by the Board of Trade being thick branches arranged irregularly on which one has to climb. But that plan suits the black man and the bridge though very shaky is a very creditable production to black engineers. This whole Songwe valley is very superior to any district I have yet seen. Of course it is impossible to speak absolutely about its healthfulness for Europeans but speaking from comparison with Chirenji there can be no doubt that unless for some very exceptional circumstance the climate is similar. The level of the valley is lower but the hills abound in flat spots where sites could easily be had. There will always be water power available from the Songwe. It is in a very good position to found the mission so that it may be in that relative geographical position to the Coy which I would like to see and which I think so necessary. Just at Chingwas the Kasaya stream enters the Songwe. The path home passes near it most of the way but I collapsed very soon after we started and had to be carried in a *machila* ...

March 8

This forenoon was somewhat dull and about midday the rain began to descend in torrents and we had an inch of it before the day was done so I had to content myself indoors practising hymns for the service at night, writing a bit of this journal and reading a little but was too unsettled to find any good in anything and the day was very unprofitable for me.

March 11[94]

... soon reached the Rukuru. I went to the place where we had crossed on the way up and found it looking very difficult and alligators shoving their ugly noses about 400 yards further down. I bribed a native to go across and return to pilot the road and the crossing turned out very easy after all. There was only one bit mouth deep. I didn't wish to be washed away to the alligators so had the assistance of a Zoku over the worst bit and then swam.

March 14 (at Karonga)

McE refers to Munro apprehending two boys who had been pilfering ... I daresay it would have been a case of flogging all round had not the steamer hove in sight ... the *Ilala* has gone on to the lagoon and Mr. Monteith bounced in on us about 9 oclock. He brings provisions and cloth for all, but naturally has lined his own nest very well ... I

---

[94]   Munro was at Bandawe for all of this month and up to 7 April when he leaves for Angoniland.

have letters from Robert, Jas, and Mary of 1st and 4th December and enclosed in one from Jeannie of 22 January. Others from Mary 17 December, mother 23rd, and a photo of Willie Nyasa.[95] I had also a letter from Duncan of 22 January and a long letter from Mrs Moir giving me recipes for making scones. The bits of news are Jas. change to Bradford, Black Watson's death, Jeannie's going home, and politically the best and most hopeful news I have heard for a while—Ministers and opposition conferring together and coming to an agreement for the good of the nation. I read everything before going to sleep including 5 'Pall Malls' and the November issue of the Geographical Proceedings. It contains a part of O'Neill's journey with laborious observations for fixing positions.

March 17

The bunks on this old steamer are not nearly as comfortable as sleeping on the seat which we did on the way up and I hardly slept a wink all night and was glad to see day. M was at the wheel all night and came in for a rest at 6. We had a head wind from the south all night so we were some distance from Deep Bay by the time I went out. I went out on deck to see the sunrise and get my head cleared. Great banks of rain clouds were discharging themselves at different places on the lake. The sun came up through a regular rag shop of cloud remnants and streaky braids of black. The effect is beautiful as his rays gradually light up on the peaks of the range on the w. side of the lake slowly creeping down the hillside till all is illuminated ...

March 19

... reached Bandawe on *Ilala* (Morrison had to run into Nkata Bay to do repair on engines).

March 25

Munro finished my plane table today ... began plotting bearings taken at north end. Think I shall send home my map on Ravenstein's scale and reserve the 4m. to 1 inch scale for taking home complete if I may have such a satisfaction.[96]

March 26

Busy plotting all day. The result tells me not to criticise other people's maps without careful examination. I find the district rather different on paper from what it was in my mind. Had a little bow and arrow shooting at sundown. Boils on feet prevented walking or lawn tennis.

April 4

Still nursing my 'big toe' it seems to improve a little. I had thoughts when at work on the road that one could manage a little more study if on a station but I do not find it so here. On the contrary I have seldom spent a more unprofitable fortnight than the last. The

---

[95] It is surmised that this might have been a new-born nephew named after McEwan and his location.

[96] It is surprising that McEwan makes no reference to the highly contagious *kausi* (thought to be scarletina) which was prevalent among the mission schoolboys at this time, as recorded by Munro.

evenings particularly were constantly interrupted and tho' a rest I have not particularly enjoyed this visit. *McE then goes on to list of books found in the Mission Library, from Muller's 'Science of Language' to Scott's 'Meteorology'—McE obviously looking forward to getting back to work on the road.*

April 5

This was a most beautiful morning. The hill at the point prevents one from seeing the best of the morning sunrise, but the east is generally ablaze with varied tints fringing an almost all pervading gold. Looking away to the north, the hills were standing out in the blue dimness of early day—the lake calm as oil and the sky above cloudless. Truly for scenery, Bandawe excels all places I have visited in Africa ... the bell for the meeting rang at eleven o'clock. The previous night Dr. Scott asked me to address the meeting with Mr. Smith interpreting but I declined. The order of Sunday work here is prayer meeting at eight–meeting of the day—for natives at eleven—evangelising in the afternoon at nearby villages—prayer meeting for station boys at night, then meeting for Europeans in the manse at seven. The forenoon meeting today was an immense improvement as regards attendance on the two previous Sundays. Dr. Scott estimated that 600 were present ... men, women and children appear promiscuously and babies at the breast are there also. The dress is varied—some plenty, some scanty.

April 6

... The sun was barely up when the women began to troop up with the *ufa* which we had ordered to be brought for sale. It was a great scene buying it. We had mats on the ground behind Mr. McC's house into which the women threw their *ufa* and then shoved forward their empty baskets to get the few beads or pickle of salt that fell to their share. They got rather uproarious and so many empty baskets were presented that we began to suspect them of having brought empty baskets for the purpose and I daresay some of them might have refilled them from the big heap, so the always necessary system had to be devised and Munro marshalled the women and then all things were done decently ...

McE and Munro had long meeting with the men - arguments about how much payment in cloth to chief and to men in advance—how long the men were to remain at the end of day and getting back to their gardens—worried about going via Angoni land—challenged by Europeans on their weak hearts when some indicated they would not go over the hills—McE and Munro said that they would take care of them.

... Mr. Munro got off at 3.15 with 75 men and everybody in good humour. I am thankful that all has gone well so far. *(There were 150 men in total—they obviously split between Munro and McEwan—but in succeeding days they had trouble with men accepting hill routes and entering Ngoni land, even threatening a chief who refused a guide that they would stay in his village and take his food for the whole gang. At one point, when a group refused, Munro called their leader a slave, which had the desired effect.*

April 9

... just after camping we were somewhat alarmed to see a line *ulendo* of Angoni men with their crowns and shields and spears file past us—there were also among them lots of Atonga and Atumbuka. Our men got very excited and began to accuse the Angoni of attempting to savage their homes so the Angoni man ordered his followers on to a hill and we got our fellows backed off a bit and then had a friendly talk with the chief ... they looked formidable, but we had more men and did not require to fear much.

April 11

McE arrives at mission (Njugu) headed by Dr. Elmslie, near Mombera's[97] village ... Dr. Elmslie is taking meteorological observations, mapping and fixing heights, so we may look for better 'scientific results' from this branch of the Livingstonia Mission than from any other.

April 12

A year today since I left Natal ...

April 13

Munro was too ill to move so McE delayed departure for another day, spent the day organising food ... notes that buying with cloth here is very extravagant and beads would be much cheaper ... We had debated in our minds the propriety of visiting Mombera in case he might take a notion to stop us and also because we were quite unable to spare cloth for a big present. However we learned that prints were well liked so laid aside 8 fathoms for the chief and as Mr. Koyi said it would be better if we went to see him, Dr. & Mrs Elmslie, Sutherland, Mr. K. myself all went over about two o'clock ... found him squatted on the top of a high ant hill inside an empty kraal with a few men about him cooking nyama for their lord and master. We were out of all ceremony and sat down on the hill. He handed us round a bit of beef of which we took a bite or two and then talked with Mr. Koyi a bit—called me an unfaan a boy, etc., etc., and gave him the present. He rather liked the cloth but some odd trinkets which I took were more highly prized—a chain—a ring—two coins—two brooches. He is a 'big wean' and likes toys. But he is also very cute. Talked of our white skins, laughed at Mr. Sutherland who is very white—said I was darker—girls might have me or Mr. Koyi, but never the others. I was surprised at putting my sunburnt arm next to Mr. Koyi's to find as dark as his. ... We had some Atonga with us whom M tried to frighten, telling them he was coming some day ... M wants men and cattle and fights for them where they can be had ...

I now write many days after the above date and think a little more detail may not be out of place. It was the first occasion on which I gave a present without receiving one in return—also it was most unusual to be allowed to sit on the dirt without mat or shade. When coming away he called on us to run, which we all did except Mr. Munro rather an undignified proceeding—in short the whole mission lacks dignity and wanting that I question the possibility of a convincing success among a people who have as much

---

[97]   Mombera's is the modern M'mbelwa's.

dignity as the Mangoni are said to have. Mombera gets the name of cleverness—his humour is undoubted and his cleverness needs to be great where he only has the mission policy to deal with. For the time the station has been at work there is no great external result to shew for the labour extended, but no doubt a great step has been made in aquatinting the natives with the character and arms of the missionaries but I am inclined to think that very large sacrifices have been made and that they have failed to affect the mind of the people beyond inducing an indifferent and limited toleration of the white man's presence and work.

I cannot bring myself to believe that after they have learned our purpose and still treat our advances with coolness that it is our duty to persist. They are a troublesome tribe and are held in dread by other tribes covering an immense area and were they subdued by the gospel or gunpowder an increased quietness in their neighbourhood would be the result. They have had a good chance of the former and rejected it. Why not withdraw and confine operations to the Lake tribes and let the Angoni understand that we will fight if attacked. I believe the breaking of the Angoni war-spirit would be comparatively simple especially as it is only in spirit that they excel their enemies - and not in numbers or physique.

April 14
McE refers to setting out, leaving his boy at the mission, and saying goodbye to Mrs. Koyi and Mrs Scott—McE complains of having very bad feet and having to cut the toes out of his canvas shoes to make them more comfortable, while Munro is still ill.

April 16
Attacked by a swarm of bees which the men had disturbed seeking honey.

April 17
As in other villages, people alarmed thinking the party was of Angoni ...

April 18
McE refers to a good reception by a very hospitable chief, Chama, who was well disposed to Europeans, which is to the credit of the influence of John Moir, the first visitor. Refers also to his Chinyanja having reached the level where he could exchange a small joke or two with the men ... while sitting outside, I indulged in some brandy and water—the first for 8 months in case of chill after our damp walk. *Angrily admonished the men for their noise*—even 21 miles doesn't tire their legs enough to quieten their tongues.

April 19
I cannot forget that this is an anniversary of Lord Beaconsfield's death and I desire much to have some degree of his persistency of purpose and, if so be, of his success in life and in the work I undertake ... If an African traveller wishes to enjoy somewhat of the quiet and rest and thought which are associated with Sunday let him pitch camp as far from a village as possible—away in the forest or among the hills—far from the madding crowd.

Life here convinces me of an inability to live independent of external circumstances. Even 120 men sleeping close to one's tent is bother enough and more in abundance to try a weary man's temper, and I must admit to giving a rough reception to someone who shoved in his head before sunrise wanting medicine. He got a snarl of 'endu ku blazes' I fear or something equally unparliamentary. When daylight had come in I lay reading 'Dodd's Parables'. They are most enjoyable and more important, beneficial but I long for our quiet sunny Sabbaths 'on the road' with Robertson and Brighton for my sermon and my home letter for meditation. My feet have been very bad for some time and yesterday's walk did little to improve them.

... *meeting the chief McE records* Mr. M got a seat near the chief and I got a very good raised seat on a mat—I didn't bother about who the people think is boss and I daresay they believe Munro is as he has beard and moustache and does most of the talking. Soon the people began to gather round ... of course the first question was 'Is your life good?' When Mr. Moir was here in 1879 the chief was not able to walk very far ... The presence of the white man at Mombera's is well known here and everybody expresses delight that the white man should have come to their country. All about here there is the same cry of fear for the Angoni tho' they say there have been no raids since Mr. Moir was here. The tsetse fly is very abundant and the consequent absence of cattle is a fair explanation of the want of Angoni raids ... we always tell the people not to fear the Angoni but to fight them bravely. I can hardly believe that anything but a thorough licking will quell them and allow peace to surrounding tribes. Like E D Young[98] I incline extremely to a policy of action both as regards slavery and the disquiet caused by the customs of the Angoni.

April 20 *McE details the extreme frustration at the delays in negotiations in getting guides for the next stretch—a frequent problem—refers to the slowness of Africans. McE gets into a fever over exasperating delay.*

... I felt better at getting (to camp) and after tea read a little of a book called Seedtime in Kashmir which is a short biography of its first medical missionary, Dr. Elmslie. I fear I can never attain to that degree of Christianity and love to Christ which persists in sending texts, prayers, and extasies of love in all letters and in generally making the religious side of life of one so prominent. And yet perhaps it is wrong of one to speak of our religious side as if assuming a two-facedness in this world, but in the meantime I love most to keep the religious feelings and thoughts inside and only parade my own conduct as it may have been affected. Dr. Elmslie seems to have been a very sensible man, but the life promises the usual tale of overwork and early death and if a man's

---

[98]   E.D. Young was the Royal Navy lieutenant who had been the very able captain of Livingstone's vessel, the *Pioneer* and was for a time temporary head of the early Livingstonia Mission. In his expedition to confirm Livingstone's death, he had been the first to carry his vessel round the impassable Murchison Cataracts.

Christianity can't make him look after his own body in a sensible way what can it do for his soul which is so much more unknowable.

But these thoughts are written just as the thoughts occur without any consideration of their justice, truth, rightness or wickedness. I sometimes wish that there was even the possibility of my ever dying from hard work. My God and only father grant grace and counsel to me and direct my ways here and elsewhere—give me a strict sense of justice on which to build a life like Christ's—make me to know my duty and give me strength to do it now and in future years so that all may tend to increase good in this thy beautiful earth. Thou alone knowest the future and I trust in thee in Christ. Our camp was two miles west of the hills tonight and we were only distant from Kambombo's (?) about 7.35 miles. *(Later next day refers to crossing a large stream called Ruwumbu - one of the principal western tributaries of the Luangwa)*

April 21

Anniversary of my arrival at Quilimane and here is my first year gone and I am well and hearty and for all kind guarding of those at home and of myself I am always thanking my Leader. *Refers later to plenty of hippo and crocs in the river they cross—promise men to hunt them for food if they succeed in spotting any—they need meat as the rations are frugal.*

April 23

There is no doubt that the people all along here realise the advantage that the presence of the white man is or would be to them. *Describes difficulty in getting the food the chief promised, and sent back a message saying that the white man would come back—according to the chief the women wouldn't grind the corn, to which McE asked if the women were the chiefs here. McE and Munro themselves did not have much food, with tea and sugar both finished and they were now using tinned coffee and milk, and the salt almost finished.*

April 24

In the valley of the Luangwa—because of sore feet, McE mainly in machila—arrived that night at the junction of Chirumbi to the west and the Kamimbi to the east.

April 26

... we had a view of the range of hills which Mr. Bain and I descended when on our Pangalla trip ... we began to feel that we were getting near Mwini Wanda's.

April 27

We were off this morning at 6.45 expecting at least to see if not reach M. Wanda ... precipitous mountains to the north west.

April 28

Shivers and fever - reached Mr. Bain's house in *machila* at midday. Found Mr. Bain's house in the usual disarray but he seems to like that.

April 29

Mr. Monteith arrived from the lake in the afternoon - the first step in his second journey to Tanganyika. Arranged with him at night regarding cloth and beads—the former lent to the Coy and the latter taken from the Coy from our boxes under cover of a permission to use our provisions. Mr. M. has not been 'straight' in the matter—in future I cannot but be suspicious. The road and the Coy are not fated to sail well in company.

May 3

Reached Karonga ... the station looks untidy just now and with unfinished houses and overgrowth. The lake has encroached on the bank a good deal since we were here last.

May 5

Both McE and Munro seedy.

May 6

... Suppurating hell began to develop this morning—hope it won't disable me.

May 7

My heel was worse than usual this morning so I gave up all work and went in for hot poulticing and resting it all day. Much matter seemed to have gathered ... about midday Mr. Munro came in hurriedly from the store where he had been working and before he could get into bed properly was seized with one of the worst shivers I have seen in Africa—almost speechless and besides the fever he was very bad with jaundice, then came sickness and restlessness and the vomiting induced great weakness and at night he was seriously ill. As long as people here have only fever here or biliousness their friends can usually treat them as well as a doctor, but in anything beyond these there is always hesitancy on treating the invalid owing to ignorance of the disease and its cause and all efforts are turned towards this, that, and the other thing to give relief whereas there is probably one mode of treatment which if persevered in would soon be efficacious but of course we didn't know what it is. It is when a serious illness like this arises that we think most of the benefit of having medical advice within easy hail.

May 8

Mr. Munro ... was very very yellow all over in the morning and very weak. During the day he got a little liebig and further on some chicken tea and relished them, but he was often sick and in pain in the stomach. *McE goes onto describe M's illness but his last written words are* ' I have been reading and enjoying Mrs. Oliphant's *Life of Edward Irving*. He seems to have been an earnest man with imaginative hopes.' [99]

---

[99]   McEwan's diary ends at this point.

Post Mortem: A Burst of Tears

With McEwan apparently too unwell to maintain his diary, Munro continues

May 12
We were both confined to our beds, Mr. Nicoll being the only person able to move about, and I am sorry to say that he is not such a gifted nurse as Mr. McEwan, he propounds many theories, but rather loathe to act on them.

May 13
Two men were sent to Mr. Bain for fruit, biscuits, or anything else that we could eat, as we have nothing of our own but the very coarsest of food, flour and tinned meats.

May 14
I am slowly gathering strength, able to take a little soup, Mr. McEwan weaker. My dog Mac died.

May 18
Mr. McEwan still very weak and hoarse with cold. I put a mustard poultice on his back and chest, which seemed to ease his cough a little ... I was up most of the day and felt very tired in the evening.

May 20
I had a very restless night as Mr. McEwan was continually shouting out through his sleep and I could not tell whether he was asleep or awake till I rose and looked ...

May 21
Mr. Nicoll sat up all night buying ivory, he bought over 200lbs weight of good ivory. Mr. McEwan very restless during night, he was shouting out a great deal—I got very little sleep ...

May 22
... He (*McEwan*) seemed to have a vacant gaze, and he is very often unconscious. He got a dose of Dr. Elmslie's mixture in the morning and another in the evening to stop his diarrhoea, his nose is often bleeding, the result is that his mouth is often clotted with blood so I clean his mouth out with warm water and florline (?) ...

May 23
Mr. McEwan very restless during the night, he has now been unconscious for the last 3 or 4 days. I got little or no sleep with him, so I feel quite worn out ... Dysentery started this afternoon, he passed nothing but pure blood, the smell was most revolting - I had to change my bed to the next room. ... while I was giving beads to the men for their food,

he got up in bed, ordered the boy away, I came running in only in time to see him fall in , the corner. He was not hurt as far as I could learn. His nose took a dreadful turn of bleeding, he would not allow me to plug his nose with cotton, he gave in by partly forcing him, it has not bled since. He seemed to turn so weak when the nose was running that I thought he was near his last. His great want is to get home ...

May 24

Mr. McEwan had 3 or 4 very bad stools in the fore part of the night, passing great lumps of clotted blood, having a most offensive smell. I had only to get up 7 or 8 times during the night, the men watched him very well ... at 3 pm His breathing became much fainter, I watched him closely and at 3.15 pm he breathed his last—he died without the slightest struggle. He has been unconscious for the last 4 or 5 days. I asked him several times if there was any message he would like to send to his mother, but he generally answered that he was going to write a lot himself, and if I had to write when the steamer would come, he would require to dictate, so he in this way always put it off. He had no idea himself

William McEwan's grave

that he was dying, this is generally the case in this country. For 12 hours or so before his death his breath had a most offensive smell. I at once despatched two men to inform Mr. Bain of the sad occurrence. I then took 7 or 8 men with me and went down to the other graves, and set them to dig the 3rd grave under the same baobab tree. I am still so weak that it was with difficulty that I managed back home. By the time I returned the body was stiff and began to smell badly. I got the body rolled in the mattress and blankets, then in the fly of my tent. My heart seemed to break within me when I saw his face covered, he who was so young and healthy looking only a fortnight ago, and to be now a stiff piece of clay. I was clear overcome and had to go to a quiet corner and had out a burst of tears which gave me great relief.

The men, poor fellows, tried to do their best to please – if I went to do anything, 2 or 3 of them would do it for me and tell me to sit down. When the body was tied up and slung on to a bamboo, the men walked quietly away with it in their hands. They went at a very slow pace so that I could keep up to them with ease. There would be about 80 of the men at the funeral, by the time we got to the grave, it was not deep enough ... but many willing hands soon put it down to six feet deep. We lowered the body into the grave at 6.15 pm. The sun was set but we had sufficient light from the bright horizon, but ere we got the grave closed, the night fell on us, and we had to find our way home in the dark. After supper, I gave 2 of his old shirts to the men that watched him the previous night, and a pair of sleeping trousers to each of the men that watched him today. How uncertain life is, who can tell when the hour of their departure may come. Let us all be ready that we may not be surprised when our summons may come.

May 25

I got the house thoroughly cleaned out, I did little else all day. Had a visit from Kasingula, hardly spoke to him. Feel a peculiar loneliness, and still I know not why. As I can scarcely believe that Mr. McEwan has gone to his eternal rest, I feel as if he were only away on a few days journey. But alas he is gone, never again to return.[100] We must all go in like manner. And oh may I live as I would like to die, trusting in the finished work of Christ.

At the end of May, Munro writes to Stevenson to tell him of his intention to carry on the work of the road 'as if Mr. McEwan was alive' and by mid-June he is lining out the new road. (He has problems with at least one chief who objects to the road going through his people's vegetable gardens, and Munro is obliged to compensate him for this.) However by the end of the month, although he is busy, he is feeling homesick and 'is longing to get out of this country.' Later after a bout of sickness and fever, saying 'I felt so miserable could I get a chance of leaving there and then for home, I think I would get all right, when anything goes wrong with me now, I feel so depressed in spirit that I have heart for nothing.' Some of this is expressed in his first real bout of temper at his men, striking one of them over the head with his umbrella, but due to fever, 'it left me trembling for near an hour afterward.' By the middle of July he is down with dysentery, and his depression could not have been improved by hearing of the death of several of the LMS missionaries in the north from the same affliction.

His condition must have become apparent to John Moir, when on the 22nd of July he was advised to leave the country at once, to which Munro reluctantly agreed. He does however make his feelings known on the treaties of annexation which are being rapidly negotiated by the Company with a number of chiefs, saying that they are signing away their country 'for a few yards of calico...in a year or two when they come to realise what they have done it will cause a great

---

[100] However, Munro perpetuated his memory by naming his tenth child—who coincidentally became an engineer—after his colleague, with the full name 'William Ottawa McEwan Munro' although he may have regretted this with the latter's premature death in 1923 at the age of 21.

ado, if not bloodshed.' He himself witnesses such a negotiation, when the chief was given a Union Jack flag to display 'only given to prevent Serpo Pinto who is now on his way to annex the eastern shore of Lake Nyassa as Portuguese territory. On his way down to Quilimane, he meets Mr. James Stevenson at Bandawe on 27 of July out on a tour of inspection—the only reference ever found by this editor to such a visit by the road's sponsor in a tantalisingly brief reference. At Mandala there was an auction sale of the effects of Stewart, Pulley and McEwan, the latter's goods realising over £40. Typically Munro records precisely that for £2.5/6d he bought a good suit! He gives a detailed account of his voyage to Natal and his stay in South Africa before arriving back in Plymouth on the 5th October 1885.

Donald Munro and family after return to Scotland

On his return to Scotland, Munro established a successful boat and house building business at Ardrishaig at the western end of the Crinan Canal, not far from his own birthplace. A few months after his return he married and subsequently raised a large family, several of whom died at a relatively young age, including William Ottawa McEwan Munro, who died in his 21st year. It was said that Munro wanted to return to Africa, but his wife was against this. In the event, Munro became a pillar of his local community, rendering service on school boards, etc. and died in 1940 at the age of 82.

Between them, Stewart, Munro and McEwan had completed construction of the road to Mweniwanda, beyond which there was a good native walking track to Lake Tanganyika, although it took a further 20 years before the road could be said to be completed, interrupted as it was by the Arab Wars of 1887-95. They had made their contribution to a route of 1400 miles from the ocean, 260 miles of this overland, fulfilling the dream of linking one of the great waterway systems of the world.

After Munro's departure, work continued sporadically on the road and by 1890, it had penetrated 10 miles beyond Mweniwanda. However, progress was interrupted by the so-called Arab Wars from 1887-89, when the slavers supported by local tribesmen attacked the Wankonde tribe, which would have been a rich source of slaves, and subsequently the ALC station at Karonga itself. For a time there was the prospect of having to abandon the north end – at least temporarily – to the attackers, and it was not until October 1889, after over two years of conflict, that a peace was negotiated after several organised assaults on the well-defended Arab stockades. This contretemps not only caused consternation in Glasgow and with the British Government, but cost the ALC dearly in terms of lost trade and the additional expenses of the war.

For a number of years, there had been discussion about a telegraph line running the length of Africa, from the Cape to Cairo, and in 1892, the great imperialist Cecil Rhodes formed the Transcontinental Telegraph Co, by which time a British Protectorate had been established over Nyasaland. In 1896 the road from Fort Hill (Chitipa) to Fife in Tanganyika was started by the British South Africa Company to provide for the construction of the telegraph over the plateau. This was built as far as the south end of L. Tanganyika by 1899, which could hardly have been accomplished without the Stevenson Road which it paralleled. This enabled the large quantities of materials to be transported, while the ALC steamboats carried both posts and wire up the Lake Nyasa, at a cost of £35,000.

There had been hopes that the Cape to Cairo railway—which was never more than a joining up of disparate lines—would continue on through Nyasaland, but the finding of large reserves of coal at Wankie in Northern Rhodesia (Zambia) coupled with the building of the railway through the Congo pre-empted this. In any case, there never was a real prospect of the railway being constructed along Lake Nyasa with its difficult topography. However, the improvement of the Stevenson Road generated increased use, with an average of 9 waggons operating by the turn of the century. There was a further improvement along sections of the road during World War I to allow for the movement of British troops, vehicles and equipment, but thereafter its use declined and much of the road fell into disrepair. It was in fact the construction of the railway from Beira to Lake Nyasa via Blantyre which effectively ended James Stevenson's dream, since this largely superseded the use of both the waterway system, and therefore the connecting road, as a main commercial artery.

However, it is acknowledged that the construction of the Stevenson Road had not unimportant consequences. First, although commercially it never achieved its predicted potential, it shifted the focus of both the Livingstonia

Mission and the ALC towards the undeveloped north of Nyasaland.[101] Secondly, it had political consequences insofar as the road, despite its primitive nature, helped to persuade the British Government to negotiate changes in the treaties with Germany in 1889-90 concerning the extent of Tanganyika, to include the road and thus fix the present boundaries of the country which was to become Malawi. At one point, the road was actually diverted to ensure that the important British government station of Fife was clearly placed within the protectorate of Nyasaland and not within the then German-administered Tanganyika.

The James Stevenson Memorial prior and after it collapsed in 2003

Parts of the road have now been incorporated into the modern system of roads, but only sections of the original can be identified, as a result of regrowth and collapse. At Silu Hill, near Mpata, a substantial memorial in the form of an Ionic cross was erected, made out of stone quarried near Karonga, and carved by local craftsmen, in honour of James Stevenson, but also with side panels acknowledging the contributions of both James Stewart and William McEwan. In recent times, this memorial has unfortunately col-

---

[101] Today, the ALC continues to operate successfully in the field of communications of a very different kind - as one of the largest on-line Internet providers in Africa.

lapsed, possibly due to local earth tremors and discussions are being held regarding its restoration. Perhaps this publication will perpetuate also the name of Donald Munro as a more durable memorial to those Scots who made their own very distinctive contribution to the development of communications in Malawi.

The Stevenson Road from Silu Hill in 2003

Appendices

Appendix 1

From the *Free Church Monthly* October 1, 1885

Another Missionary Martyr

32

was dying, this is generally the case in this country for 12 hours or so before his death, his breath had a most offensive smell. I at once despatched 2 men to inform Mr Bain of the sad occurrence. I then took 7 or 8 men with me and went down to the other graves, and set them to dig the 3rd grave under the same baobab tree, I am still so weak that it was with difficulty that I managed back home. by the time I returned the body was stiff and began to smell badly. I got the body rolled in the mattress and blankets, then in the fly of my tent. My heart seemed to break within me when I saw his face covered, he who was so young and healthy looking only a fortnight ago, and to be now a stiff piece of clay. I was clean overcome and had to go to a quiet corner and had out a burst of tears which gave me great relief. The men poor fellows tried to do their best to please. If I went to do anything 2 or 3 of them would do it for me and tell me to sit down. When the body was tied up and slung on to a bamboo, the men walked quietly away with it in their hands, they went at a very slow pace so that I could keep up to them with ease, there would be about 80 of the men at the funeral, by the time we got to the grave, it was not deep enough at the men, but many willing hands soon put it down 6 feet deep we lowered the body into the grave at 6.15 P.M. The sun was set but we had sufficient light from the bright horizon, but ere we got the grave closed night fell on us. and ...

Abstract from Donald Munro's Diary describing McEwan's death

On the 4th June last the *Ilala* arrived at our central mission port of Bandawe from the North end of Lake Nyasa, with the sad intelligence of the death of Mr. W. O. McEwan, C.E. as reported by telegraph in our last. He was tenderly nursed by Mr. Donald Munro, himself an invalid, from whose pathetic letter and journal, sent to the sorrowing mother of our missionary-engineer, we compile this brief narrative.

Mr. McEwan had completed his most successful season of work on the Stevenson Road from Nyasa to Tanganyika, and had returned to Bandawe following Mr. Munro, the carpenter and evangelist, to prepare for the second season, and to enable Mr. Munro, then fever-stricken, to recruit. He himself had suffered no sickness, and was full of enthusiastic hope and faith in God. He resolved to return to the road, not direct by the steamer, but by a roundabout land route, so as to visit the Angoni station to the west and Mr. Bain at Mwiniwanda or Chirenji to the north. He and Mr. Donald Munro, with 120 natives for road work, left Bandawe on the 7th. April. His feet were still blistered by the much tramping of which Dr. Livingstone complained, and he had to be carried for a few days. After 2 days beside Dr. Elmslie, Mr. Koyi, and Mr. Williams on the hills, the party reached the comparatively healthy station of the Rev. A. Bain on the 28th. April. His feet were not better, and both he and Mr. Munro were very feverish.

Nevertheless they set out for the most difficult portion of the road, on the rocky ascent from Nyasa, where Mr. James Stewart fell victim to his loved duty. Mr. Munro was the first to require treatment for his old ailment, bilious fever and jaundice. But for Mr. McEwan's nursing during the first three days of the attack, it would have proved fatal. Both were suffering from diarrhoea, which a mixture supplied by Dr. Elmslie when they set out stopped in Mr. Munro's case. Mr. McEwan however, never recovered from it. On Sabbath, 10th May he took to bed, when Mr. Munro was able to rise and become nurse in his turn. On the 12th both were down, and on the 13th 'two men were sent to Mr. Bain for some sweet biscuits, as we have nothing but coarse food.' Mr. Munro became stronger, and on the 16th on a calm and clear morning 'all ventured down to the lake for a bath; after which Mr. McEwan went back to bed.' From Sabbath the 17th. May he seems to have lain in a hopeless condition, much comforted by Mr. Munro's tender care and the supplies sent by Mr. Bain, but soon became very delirious. His duty was ever in his mind, and he shouted through one long night for the men and boys to set to work. Neither medicine nor eatable food, all of which he took, had any effect. Mr. Munro was worn out by sleepless watching, and sent for Mr. Bain. On Sabbath afternoon the 24th May, the sufferer quietly breathed away his spirit free from pain, and without a message for his loved ones, since to the last he expected to be able to dictate a letter. 'He spoke of having a great deal to write home before the steamer came.' The place was Karonga's on the far shore, where they seem to have been waiting for the steamer.

'I at once' writes Mr. Munro, 'sent to Mr. Bain telling of the sad news, then took a number of the men and went down to dig a grave, under the big baobab tree, alongside of Messrs Stewart and Gowans. I rolled him in his mattress and blankets, then in the fly of my tent. When all was ready, the men gently carried him with their hands to the grave. About eighty of the men attended the funeral, and seemed much put about, as he was a general favourite with the natives.'

The young missionary was buried after sunset. Mr. Bain arrived after a very fatiguing march of forty miles. Mr. Munro, whose term of service will expire at the close of the year, further writes that his sad death is a loss to all his friends in Africa, for his kind, caring manner drew him many friends, who lament his unexpected death.

Appendix 2

Abstract from the diary of W.O. McEwan 1883.

Monday night, 9 April 1883.

At the end of 1882, among other books I happened to be reading one by Professor Huxley on 'Science & Culture'. His books are neither well known or spoken about much in Glasgow. His name is to be regarded as one to be united with Tyndall's and others in a class of unchristian Scientists, or at least holding views not generally admired by the 'unco guid.' Considering the feeling with which I was unconsciously possessed it came as a pleasant surprise to find in the above book sentences delightful in their practical sense, and large-hearted in their expressions towards the Bible, if not towards Christianity, in its wider sense. My mind at this time was running much on Africa, and the work to be accomplished there in exploration and civilization. That Continent has always fascinated me.

The map of Africa was my favourite at school, perhaps because it was so easily drawn. The geography of Africa I always knew best – perhaps because at that time most of the Continent was marked 'unknown'. When schooldays were – alas – past, and geography became a recreation instead of a task the charm was not lessened. The name of Livingstone completed the spell, and from admiration to desire for imitation there is but a thought, and my ideal life has ever been 'Livingstone's work, Livingstone's religion, and Beaconsfield's perseverance, and God's help.' The establishment of Livingstonia may be said to have marked the time when my interest deepened and became more intelligent. That was somewhere about '75, and since then I have mentally turned to Africa weekly if not daily. As in all other matters there have been times of less or more enthusiasm, the former when engrossed in more immediate matters demanding much mental attention—the latter when any explorer returned with new discoveries won hard, or when attracted to a study in detail of African work when preparing a map or paper. But a man cannot always be *thinking* about practical questions – if his interest is sincere, his desire deep, his heart bold, a crisis must always present itself in which he will have to decide whether he means to *work*. For me this approaches.

In August next my articles expire and I must decide soon whether I mean to go on in the present groove, or to acquire the special knowledge necessary for an efficient explorer in Africa. For many this is an extremely simple question. They have time and money in plenty. The only item of which I have sufficient is inclination for the work. The money and therefore the time, might be found, and if I were sure that I had the perseverance and sense of purpose to go through the work properly I would not hesitate to ask or borrow, but I doubt it much—very much. Want of perseverance means opportunities lost, and I feel almost that this is the rock that will be fatal to my life's work. It may be said that a person has perseverance in sin, but sin is so easy, it needs none. When I think of all this it makes me despond, but throwing it off for the time and remembering only Africa, recollecting also the general knowledge displayed in Prof. Huxley's book, on the 28 March I penned a letter.

28 March '83

Dear Sir,

I am preparing to take part in the work of exploring and opening up Central Africa. With this end in view I have spent the last six years learning my regular profession of a 'Civil and Mining Engineer'. Until this time the practical parts of my business have absorbed most of my attention, at the expense of the scientific. I am quite aware of how useless an unscientific explorer must prove, and on the expiry of my articles next August I purpose tuning to this part of my preparation, and write now to ask if you would be kind enough to advise me on the following questions.

Would you recommend me to take a complete science course at some University—studying all the branches ? or

To take up one branch only, and make a separate or special study of it ? If so which would be the most useful for an African explorer?

I do not care for degrees, and am anxious rather to be ready for work as soon as is consistent with efficiency.

To have many letters of this type would prove a nuisance, and I can only plead the importance of the work I anticipate and the sincerity of my purpose as grounds for expecting you to take the trouble to answer my enquiry.

I am

Yours faithfully
Wm. O. McEwan

And on the 30th received a distinct and courteous reply, which I will always treasure as showing what always should be the attitude of those who have attained to those who have not, be they who they may.

Office of HM Inspector of Fisheries
Mar. 30/1883

Dear Sir,

On the face of the matter, I should be disposed to advise you not to take a complete science course in preparation for your proposed African work, but to devote all the time you can give to acquiring

1. A sound practical knowledge of the principles of Zoology, Botany and Geology, and
2. Skill in making meteorological and magnetical observations.

It would take time to discuss the whys and wherefores of this in a letter, but if you can make it convenient to call on me any afternoon next week, at the address which heads my note, between 3 and 5 in the afternoon, I shall be very glad to talk the matter over with you.

Fifty per cent of the letters I receive <u>are</u> unmitigated nuisances but I hold it to be a duty as well as a pleasure to place such experience as I possess at the disposition of any one who has a serious and practical purpose in life.

I am,

Yours very truly
T. Huxley

As invited in that note I called on the professor with the following result.

Leaving my office at 9 Victoria Chrs. Westminster, at half past three on Wednesday the 4th April I took my way slowly past the scene of the explosion which Londoners make so much of, to the Home Office where I was directed by the Hall Porter to the Office of H.M. Inspector of Fisheries. I made my way to Room 17, and bound myself to go through the interview by knocking at the door. A distinct 'come in' summoned me inside, and on opening I found that the voice was Prof. Huxley's. He was alone. The first glimpse of one whom we know not by sight generates peculiar feelings. Imaginings may be verified, oftener they are shattered. Instead of the grey hairs there may only be the youthful colour. The piercing eye may only be dull. The intelligent features may turn out of a commonplace cast – the manly carriage of a man of 'fame' may be only a shuffling gait. The dignity, pride and reserve of the great man may after all turn out to be kindness, courtesy and condescension.

I had seen photographs of Professor Huxley, and though they did not appear as they shewed him it was easy to recognize the man. Heaven save everybody from writing 'Carlyleian Reminiscences' but I cannot refrain from describing the Professor as he appeared to me. He is not nice looking, and any intellect appears only in the eyes—there is certainly none of it in his dress—very 'baggily' attired. But one notices none of these things when he speaks; his conversation and his books are very similar—remarkably pure in composition unmistakably distinct in meaning—and entirely devoid of any attempts at 'Ruskinite' particularly in the arrangement of words—the person would be dull indeed who did not understand the matter being explained. On mentioning my name, and thanking him for affording the interview, the professor shook hands formally offered me a seat, took his own, and in a voice that seemed to imply no mere superficial interest in my case asked, ''Well now tell me what you propose to do''. Considering that I had come to be advised on this point the demand was rather startling, but I answered by detailing briefly what my education and training had been to the present time, and my desire for African work. ''I once had thoughts of going there myself'' he said ''but I never got that length''.

''For a traveller what is wanted is that he should be able to do his travels what no other person can do better, namely to study the country in its geological and productive and other aspects. There is no direct opportunity of employing chemistry in this work, and I would not recommend you to spend time over a acquiring a complete knowledge of it. The preparation I would advise is this – Physics, Botany, Zoology, Geology and practice in making meteorological and magnetical observations. Being a civil engineer you will be sufficiently acquainted with surveying instruments. I do not think there is a better college for getting this course to suit your prospective work than the one with which I am connected at South Kensington. I say so from deliberate knowledge, and not from being connected with it myself. You have there the most complete laboratory instruction that is given in the country, and you as an engineer will have found out, perhaps to your cost, how futile book-learning is without practice. It is often more harm than good, and will serve you little purpose if you find yourself on the top of a mountain in Abyssinia with your barometer broken.

Students have the opportunity of observing at Kew. In fact they are at the headquarters of science in the country, and have therefore the greatest opportunities for gaining the fullest and best information. The time this course would take depends of course on the learner. It could be done in two years, but three would be better. Whichever time one takes the work requires intelligence, hard work and application, and to look at you I should think you have your share of these. One year at any rate would require to be devoted to a painstaking study of Geology and its connections. Then suppose you have finished your studies, what do you propose to do?"

I said I knew how difficult it was to get attached to expeditions, but I thought it would be possible to get appointed in connection with one of these and sent to some Mission Station where scientific observers are kept for these purposes solely. Prof. Huxley said there were three principal ways of getting into Africa. By the Nile, Congo, or from the South. In the first, above the places usually frequented by travelers, there is a splendid field. In the second, I expect that that district will be overrun very shortly by a sort of people among whom one would run an excellent chance of having one's throat cut. In the South one is among more civilized surroundings, and there is an equally good field for scientific exploration. Of all the explorers that have been in Africa only three or four at most, have been truly competent for scientific work, and the Germans have been the most able men.

To make a journey, discover some new river, come home and be lionized for a time by the R.G. Soc. is all very well but it has no permanent results (this I disagree with) and as for missionaries (except for the souls of the poor natives they think they convert) their work does no good. A person should never visit hot countries until he is set, and as a young man his bones and frame are never in that state until he is 22 or 23. I said that I never had any intention of doing the work at my own expense, and Prof replied that if Scientists found a man who could do work they wanted done abroad, they would perhaps send him at their expense.

At any rate the course he had recommended was the best, and if I took it and at Kensington he would see that I had every chance of acquiring the special knowledge that would suit my purpose. I said that I had thought of Edinburgh University. The Professor seemed to think it a good one but there is want of efficient laboratory practice and he thought Kensington was the best. He would send me a prospectus (It was a government business so they did not require to toady for fees) and if I decide to follow his advice I am first to go to him, and he will see me started in the subjects that will suit my purpose. I hoped he wouldn't think I had taken too much liberty in coming to him, but he said he was always glad to assist anyone who had an earnest purpose and meant to do good work.

And so I left charmed with the Professor's courtesy, clearness and kindness, assured that he was essentially a scientific man and not commercial, and rather uncertain as to what his religious tenets are. After all this my opinion at the present time is that I should stick at the engineering for another year, during which I must tackle the German and overcome the mathematics and then in October '84 begin the course which Prof. Huxley indicated – do it in two years if possible, at most in three. I will then be as he says 'set', and if I work as hard as I ought to have done, by that time I may expect to be able to do 'good work', and thus not disappoint those who have taken some interest in my preparation. The finances of this business are my greatest trouble, and the want of them might prevent me from doing anything of this study that I contemplate. Hitherto a Higher Mind seems to have directed, <u>has</u> directed, the course of my life in all its concerns in a manner very kind and advantageous to me and I do not fear that it will desert me now when more earnestly than ever I endeavour to do something for that great continent to which has already been devoted so much that is good and noble in the lives of my own countrymen. I would fain dedicate my best powers and thought to a work in which Livingstone's name has not yet been overshadowed.

Bibliography

Unpublished papers

African Lakes Company Archive, National Library of Scotland, Edinburgh.

John W. Moir Papers 1866-93, University of Edinburgh.

Letters of Alexander Low Bruce, National Library of Scotland, Edinburgh.

McCracken, J., "Livingstonia Mission and the Evolution of Malawi," (M.Sc; Cambridge 1967).

McEwan, W.O., "Diary for 1884-5," Royal Scottish Geographical Society, Glasgow

MacMillan, H.W., "The Origin and Development of the African Lakes Company, 1878-1908" (Ph.D.; Edinburgh 1970).

Munro, D., "Diary for 1881-85, Private Papers.

Ross, A.C., "Origin and Development of the Church of Scotland Mission, Blantyre, Nyasaland 1875-1926" (Ph.D.; Edinburgh 1968).

Thomson, W., "Glasgow and Africa: Connections and Attitudes 1870-1900," (Ph.D.; Glasgow 1970).

Wilshaw, C., "Scotland's Forgotten Graves on Lake Malawi," Private mss. (1997).

Published

Bridges, R., (ed.), *Imperialism, Decolonisation and Africa* (London, 2000).

Buchanan, J., *The Shire Highlands* (Edinburgh, 1885).

Cross, D. Kerr, "Geographical Notes of the Country between Lakes Nyassa, Rukwa and Tanganyika", *Scottish Geographical Magazine*, 6, (1890).

Drummond, H., *Tropical Africa* (London, 1889).

Fotheringham, M.L., *Adventures in Nyassaland* (London, 1891).

Free Church Monthly, (Glasgow, 1885).

Galbraith, J. S., *Mackinnon and East Africa 1878-1895: A Study in the New Imperialism* (Cambridge, 1972).

Hanna, A.J., *The Beginnings of Nyasaland and Northern Rhodesia, 1859-95* (Oxford, 1950)

Hanna, A.J., *The Story of the Rhodesias and Nyasaland* (London, 1960).

Henderson, J., "Northern Nyasaland", *Scottish Geographical Magazine* 16 1900 82-9

Hetherwick, A., *The Romance of Blantyre* (London, 1932).

Jack, J.W., *Daybreak in Livingstonia* (Edinburgh, 1901).

Laws, R., Reminiscences of Livingstonia (Edinburgh, 1924).

Livingstone, W.P., *Laws of Livingstonia* (London, 1934).

McCarthy, J., "Journey into Africa: The Life and Death of Keith Johnston;" *Scottish Cartographer and Explorer* (1844-79) (Latheronwheel, 2003).

McCracken, J.L., *Politics and Christianity in Malawi 1875-1940: The Impact of the Livingstonia Mission in Northern Province* (Blantyre[2], 2000).

MacDonald, D., *Africana: Or the Heart of Heathen Africa* (London, 1882).

McIntosh, H., *Robert Laws: Servant of Africa* (Carberry and Blantyre, 1993).

Moir, F.L.M., "Eastern Route to Central Africa", *Scottish Geographical Magazine* 1, (1885).

Moir, F.L.M., *After Livingstone* (London, 1924).

Moir, F.L.M., "The Story of the African Lakes Corporation and River Route", in Leo Wiental (ed.) *The Story of the Cape to Cairo Railway and Route from 1887 to 1922* vol.1. (London, n.d.).

Oliver, R., *The Missionary Factor in East Africa* (London, 1952).

Pachai, B., (ed.) *The Early History of Malawi*, (London, 1972).

Ransford, O., *Livingstone's Lake: The Drama of Nyasa* (London, 1966).

Ravenstein, E.G., *Explorations in the Territories of the African Lakes Company*, Proc. R.G.S. 4, (1880).

Smith, R. C., "The Africa Trans-Continental Telegraph Line," *Rhodesiana, 33*, (1975).

Stevenson, J., *The Civilisation of South Eastern Africa, including remarks on the approach to Nyassa by the Zambezi, and Notes on the Country between Kilwa and Tanganyika*, (Glasgow, 1877).

Stevenson, J., *The Water Highways of the Interior of Africa, Trans. Glasg. Phil. Soc.* (1883).

Stevenson, J., *The Arab in Central Africa*, (Glasgow, 1888).

Stewart, J., Observations on the Western Side of Lake Nyassa and on the Country intervening between Nyassa and Tanganyika, *Proc. R.G.S.* ii, (1880).

Stewart, J., Lake Nyassa, and the Water Route to the Lake Region of Africa, *Proc. R.G.S.* 5,(1881).

Stewart, J. F., The Stevenson Road and the Diary of William McEwan, Part I *Scottish Geographical Magazine* 59 1943 31- 6.

Stewart J.F., The Diary of William McEwan, Part II *Scottish Geographical Magazine* 59 1943 106-10.

Thomson, J., *To the Central African Lakes and Back: The Narrative of the Royal Geographical Society's East Central Africa Expedition, 1878 – 1880* (London, 1881).

Thompson, T.J., (ed.) *From Nyassa to Tanganyika: The Journal of James Stewart CE in Central Africa 1876-1879* (Blantyre, 1989).

Wilshaw, C., (ed.) *A Lady's Letters from Central Africa: A Journey from Mandala, Shire Highlands in 1890 by Jane F. Moir* (Blantyre, 1991).

Wientahl, L., (ed.) *The Story of the Cape to Cairo Railway*, (London, n.d.).

Wilshaw, C., Trek to Tanganyika, *The Lady*, April, 1998.

Wolf, J.B., Commerce, Christianity and the Creation of the Stevenson Road, *African Historical Studies*, IV, 2 (1971).